The Manhattan Diaries Series

Rise and Shine, Manhattan Style

Day-to-Day Luxuries You Can't Miss

Manhattan Vitality
Just Like That

The Manhattan Diaries Series

Manhattan Allure ~ Just Like That

Manhattan Vitality ~ Just Like That

Manhattan Lifestyle ~ Just Like That

Manhattan Ambition ~ Just Like That

The Manhattan Diaries Series

Rise and Shine, Manhattan Style

Day-to-Day Luxuries You Can't Miss

Manhattan Vitality
Just Like That

JAIMI TAYLOR

Urban Chronicles Publishing House
an imprint of The Ridge Publishing Group
Coeur d'Alene, Idaho, U.S.A.

DISCLAIMER: The ideas, concepts, and opinions expressed in The Manhattan Diaries Series (hereinafter referred to as "Series") are intended to help readers make thoughtful and informed decisions about their lifestyle. This Series is sold with the understanding that author and publisher are not rendering medical advice of any kind, nor is this Series intended to replace the medical advice, nor to diagnose, prescribe, or treat any disease, condition, illness, or injury. It should not be used as a substitute for treatment by or the advice of a professional healthcare provider. It is recommended that before beginning any diet or exercise program, including any aspect of the Series, you receive full medical clearance from a licensed healthcare provider. Although the author and publisher have endeavored to ensure that the information provided in the Series is complete and accurate, the author and publisher claim no responsibility to any person or entity for any liability, loss, or damage caused or alleged to be caused directly or indirectly as a result of the use, application, or interpretation of the material in this Series, or any errors or omissions in the Series.

Library of Congress Control Number: 2024923942

Taylor, Jaimi
Rise and Shine, Manhattan Style: Day-to-Day Luxuries You Can't Miss by Jaimi Taylor

ISBN: 978-1-956905-53-3 (e-book)
ISBN: 978-1-956905-52-6 (Softcover)

1. Self-Help / Motivational & Inspiration. 2. Self-Help / Personal Growth / Happiness. 3. Self-Help / Personal Success. 4. Travel / United States / Northeast / Middle Atlantic (New York). 5. Body, Mind & Spirit / Inspirational & Personal Growth. 6. Self-Help / Personal Appearance & Grooming. 7. Health & Fitness / Healthy Living. I. Title. II. Series.

First Edition: November 2024

Printed in the United States of America

Contents

The Manhattan Diaries Series

DARE TO REIMAGINE YOURSELF . . .

21 Steps to Reinvent and Discover a Side of You Manhattan's Never Seen

The Manhattan Diaries Series presents:

Manhattan Allure—Just Like That mini-series (books 1–5)

Manhattan Vitality—Just Like That mini-series (books 6–10)

Manhattan Lifestyle—Just Like That mini-series (books 11–16)

Manhattan Ambition—Just Like That mini-series (books 17–21)

Meet the Author
https://www.LAMoeszinger.com

Meet the Publisher, Urban Chronicles Publishing House
https://www.NewYouniversityChronicles.com

Step into the whirlwind world of New York's glitzy underbelly, where the scintillating secrets and laugh-out-loud confessions of a metropolitan woman are laid bare by someone truly in the know. Through essays pulled from her chic "Manhattanite's Survival Guide—Success in the City," L invites us on an unforgettable strut from her glamorous youth, through her middle-aged mazes, and into her fabulous sixties.

For the juiciest tidbits about L's life, her "Manhattan Chronicles" blog is the place to be. This blog is an unfiltered dive into L's world, from her spiritual musings to her meticulous weigh-ins to her New Youniversity Chronicles—The Manhattan Diaries series—personal tales. Dive into her cosmos at her blog site: https://www.ManhattanChronicles.com.

The Manhattan Diaries Series

Rise and Shine, Manhattan Style

Day-to-Day Luxuries You Can't Miss

Manhattan Vitality
Just Like That

Introduction: Dawn and Dazzle – Manhattan's Rituals of Radiance!

Hello, Manhattan mavens and lovers of the urban jungle! As you navigate the glamorous, fast-paced streets of New York City, have you ever wondered how to infuse a touch of luxury into your daily routine, Manhattan-style? Do you wake up in the city that never sleeps with a zest for the extraordinary, ready to seize the day like a true New Yorker? Well, dear readers, the city itself is a treasure trove of day-to-day luxuries waiting to be uncovered, and I'm here to unveil them all in "Rise and Shine, Manhattan-Style: Day-to-Day Luxuries You Can't Miss."

In this enchanting journey, I'm taking you on a guided tour through Manhattan's everyday extravagances. Success in the Big Apple isn't just about wit or navigating its bustling avenues—it's about embracing the little luxuries that make each day memorable, from savoring your morning coffee to reveling in an evening stroll through Central Park. I've traversed the city's hidden gems, indulged in its secret pleasures, and discovered the everyday luxuries that keep Manhattan's finest enchanted by their city. But remember, true luxury is a state of mind.

Consider this your exclusive invitation to a limited-edition of The Manhattan Diaries series, Manhattan-style experience. Whether you savor these everyday delights one at a time, explore them week by week, or read about them while sipping champagne on your favorite rooftop. The pace is entirely up to you. Visualize yourself immersing in a chapter during your morning coffee or dedicating a weekend to luxuriating in the entire book. Within these pages, you'll unlock the keys to infusing your daily life with the magic of Manhattan, and the radiance that follows will leave you feeling like a true urban aristocrat.

RISE AND SHINE, MANHATTAN STYLE

As we embark on this journey together, I'll be your guide, revealing how effortlessly you can embrace the charm of Manhattan in your daily life. This guide isn't just about luxury tips; it's a celebration of your spirit, your relationships, and your daily aspirations in the city. Join me in uncovering the secrets that will allow you to elevate each day, transforming the mundane into the extraordinary. I'm not just dedicated to helping you master the art of Manhattan-style living; I'm here to ignite the passion in your heart that propels you to your most luxurious self. Embrace it, and the energy of New York will be yours to command!

My passion for this city-centric guide is born from my own personal journey, filled with everyday highs and lows, moments of enchantment, and the joy of discovering Manhattan's hidden treasures. Like many city dwellers, I had to navigate the urban landscape, sometimes veering off the well-trodden path. But today, I stand before you, ready to inspire you to infuse your daily life with Manhattan's unique charm.

As time sails on the Hudson River, our life paths inevitably intersect. For me, the whirlwind of career pursuits, downtown soirees, and self-discovery converged with my love for the city, leading me to work with the Urban Chronicles Publishing House.

New York City's allure isn't just for celebrities or trust fund beneficiaries; it's accessible to everyone, whether you're a wide-eyed newcomer in your twenties or a seasoned aficionado in your sixties. Embrace this journey with me as we embark on a path to city stardom in this eighth step—The Manhattan Diaries series is a twenty-one step journey; twenty-one books to reinvent and discover a side of you Manhattan's never met.

"Rise and Shine, Manhattan-Style: Day-to-Day Luxuries You Can't Miss" equips you with the tools to not only navigate the city but also to infuse your daily life with the magic of Manhattan. I'm here as your city guardian, ensuring you realize that everything you crave starts within. Embrace Manhattan's luxuries, and watch as each day becomes a precious gem in your urban crown. If you've dreamed of experiencing Manhattan-style living, this guide is your key to unlocking its charm! I've witnessed friends rise to a Manhattan lifestyle, proving that as you align within, the city will reflect it back in opulence and everyday enchantment. That's a promise straight from the heart of New York.

Relying on The Manhattan Diaries series has always been my compass. Whenever the city threw a curveball my way, this series steered me right back to the path of everyday luxury. The allure of embracing Manhattan-style living keeps me coming back to these pages, and trust me, it's far more exhilarating than settling for the ordinary.

With every page you turn, you'll discover the blueprint, insider secrets, and the support you need to make your everyday life in Manhattan a luxurious adventure. The Manhattan Diaries series is tailored for everyone, from those seeking a fabulous urban lifestyle to social butterflies and luxury lifestyle enthusiasts.

There are countless ways to elevate your day in the Big Apple, but if you're looking for the chicest route to Manhattan-style living, it's right here in The Manhattan Diaries. Immerse yourself in its secrets while reciting positive mantras, and let the city's vibrancy elevate your everyday life; and, in this case, turning each day into a masterpiece.

Navigating the City with The Manhattan Diaries

Welcome to "Rise and Shine, Manhattan-Style: Day-to-Day Luxuries You Can't Miss." Think of this edition of The Manhattan Diaries as your personal cosmopolitan diary, as interactive as an invitation to Manhattan's most exclusive events. Each chapter is enriched with journal pages, waiting for your Manhattan musings and anecdotes. Whether you want to record the day's highlights in your "Luxury Chronicles" or delve into deep reflections in your "Luxury Confessions," these pages are yours to fill—see Cocktails and Chronicles: "Journal Pages: Pen Your Tales."

But . . .

1 Before you start penning your thoughts, take a moment to breathe. Close your eyes and, in that quiet moment, express a heartfelt "thank you" to the city that never sleeps. Feel that rush of gratitude, as if you've just discovered a hidden gem in the heart of Manhattan. Let that "thank you" resonate deep within your heart—because that, my dear readers, is the magic of Manhattan.

2 Begin by detailing the fabulous moments you've experienced since delving into the last luxurious advice you've received. Write them down under "Completed Tasks," and relish in the feeling of embracing Manhattan-style living every day.

3 Once you've celebrated your luxury triumphs, turn the page to "Action Items" and outline your aspirations for infusing even more charm into your daily life. Reflect on what's left to conquer in your journey toward Manhattan-style living, capturing your next steps in this transformational saga.

Through The Manhattan Diaries series, you'll encounter timeless "inspirational quotes" that are as iconic as Manhattan's skyline. These pearls of wisdom are your luxury mantras. Savor them, recite each word as if you're toasting at an upscale Manhattan soiree, and let them resonate deep within your urban luxury soul.

As you approach the end of each guide, you'll discover a "City Roundup." Here, you'll find a chic recap summarizing all the insider tips from your journey toward everyday luxury, ensuring you never miss a New York luxury minute.

So, get ready to rise and shine like a Manhattanite, darlings. Behind the cityscape lies a world of daily enchantment, luxury, and endless possibilities for your everyday life. It's time to embrace the charm of Manhattan and live your life in the city that never sleeps with style, grace, and everyday luxury.

INTRODUCTION

Rise and Shine, Manhattan Style: Day-to-Day Luxuries You Can't Miss

Doll faces, it's time to unwrap the beauty of the city's dawn. Introducing the eighth chic chapter of The Manhattan Diaries: "Rise and Shine, Manhattan-Style: Day-to-Day Luxuries You Can't Miss."

Ah, Manhattan mornings! Where the skyline kisses the first rays, where dreams dressed in silk robes sip their first coffees, and where the streets awaken with a promise of grandeur and glitter. This isn't just another morning routine, sweethearts. It's a curated dance of day-to-day luxuries that every Manhattan darling knows by heart.

Living large in this city isn't merely about the fabulous soirees or the sparkling champagne. Oh no, it's in those intimate moments of dawn, those private rituals of self-love, that truly transform the mundane into the magical. By cherishing yourself, you're not just altering your relationship with those pesky thoughts; you're hosting a lavish ball for them, inviting them to waltz with intention and grace.

So, whether it's a spa-like soak or a serene moment with your thoughts on a penthouse terrace, dive deep into the luscious, intentional start to every Manhattan day. Wake up, darling, and let's paint the town red . . . starting at sunrise!

Meet the Maestros Behind the Curtain

Welcome to the glittering realm of The Manhattan Diaries series, penned by an eclectic group of scribes who know how to make words shimmer just like that Midtown skyline. Each of these writers possesses the kind of Manhattan moxie that's as electrifying as a Saturday night at Studio 54. Picture the literary equivalent of the fabulous foursome from "Sex and the City," but with a little extra Manhattan mascara.

Our authors, darlings, aren't just writers; they're connoisseurs of all things NYC, dishing out stories with the precision of a Fifth Avenue stylist crafting the perfect blowout. Their tales are imbued with the kind of insider knowledge only those who've sipped martinis at the city's most secretive spots can truly understand.

So, as you delve into the pages of The Manhattan Diaries know that you're not just reading words, you're sipping on the prose of New York's finest literary mixologists. Here's to a journey as sparkling and unforgettable as a New York night out. Cheers, darling!

Behind the Scenes with the Urban Chronicles Publishing House

In the whirlwind of New York's high society, the Urban Chronicles Publishing House has emerged as the ultimate style sage for modern-day self-help. Over a cosmopolitan-fueled decade, they've become the city's go-to curators for crafting that sought-after, enviable life. The Manhattan Diaries? Envision it as your exclusive, VIP backstage pass, dripping with Upper East Side allure.

If you've ever pictured yourself sashaying through Manhattan with poise, if you've craved that skyline backdrop to your impeccable life, or if you simply seek the secrets whispered in the plush corners of the city's most exclusive clubs—The Manhattan Diaries is your ticket. Crafted under the elite banner, Urban Chronicles Publishing House, this imprint doesn't just offer you insights; it's your personal invite to the city's most glamorous circles.

> ➤ **Forever en Vogue**. Everyone, from the Wall Street moguls to the aspiring Broadway stars, dreams of basking in New York's radiant glow, of living a life drenched in style and substance. The wisdom in The Manhattan Diaries is as timeless as a Fifth Avenue romance, ensuring you're always en vogue.

INTRODUCTION

➤ **A Blueprint for the Elite**. Nestled within these pages are the golden rules of city living, from mastering the cocktail chatter to undergoing a dazzling reinvention. Whether you're a seasoned socialite, an ambitious parent, or a fresh-eyed dreamer, these guides have something to make your heart race a little faster.

➤ **The Perfect Accessory**. Their petite stature makes these guides a seamless fit for your Prada clutch or your gym tote. Think of them as your urban survival kit—a blend of wisdom and wit that's as crucial as your red lipstick for those Manhattan nights.

Take a sip of this rich concoction, and let the Urban Chronicles Publishing House unlock Manhattan, unveiling a New York you only dreamed of. Welcome to the allure of the elite, darling.

Unveiling The Ridge Publishing Group

Picture The Ridge Publishing Group as the rising star on New York's literary and entertainment horizon. Envision an eclectic empire—books, cinema, and board games—setting the stage to become the world's haute couture of theological discourse. Think Fifth Avenue for theological resources: luxurious, elite, and unparalleled.

Dive into their esteemed collections. They hold the keys to the illustrious Guardians of Biblical Truth Publishing Group and the evocative New Narrated Study Bible (NNSB) series. Delve deeper and find the Hoyle Theology Publishing Group and its opulent Hoyle Theology Encyclopedia—a treasure trove for the cerebral sophisticate. And for those who like their theology paired with a cinematic flair, there's the Documentaries in Print Publishing Group with its tantalizing series like Defending the Faith. And, of course, for those cocktail nights with a side of divine strategy, the Heaven's Seminary board games and card decks offer a chic twist.

But that's not all. The Ridge Publishing Group is more than a theological publishing powerhouse; it's a brand. Alongside its flagship, it flaunts trendy imprints: AuthorsDoor Group and AuthorsDoor Leadership (check them out at the glamorous digital boulevard of https://www.AuthorsDoor.com), the ritzy Urban Chronicles Publishing House and New Youniversity (make your reservation at https://www.LAMoeszinger.com), and the novel delights of Ethan Fox Books (sip your martini and browse https://www.EthanFox Books.com).

For a sneak peek into the world where theology meets Manhattan glamour, rendezvous at their digital penthouse: https://www.Ridge PublishingGroup.com. It's theology made chic.

A NOTE TO THE READER

Typos in this book? Errors (and inconsistencies) can get through proofreaders, so if you do find any typos or grammatical errors in this book, I'd be very grateful if you could let me know using this email address typos@LAMoeszinger.com. Thank you ☺

Penthouse Perspectives:
Sunrise Meditations Amidst Skyscrapers

Manhattan, a city that doesn't merely witness dawn—it becomes one with it. Every morning, as the sun peeks over the horizon, Manhattan's heart swells with tales of hope, dreams, and unyielding spirit. Here, amidst the forest of skyscrapers, it isn't simply about witnessing another day; it's about greeting it—with grace, elegance, and an essence of serene sophistication.

Imagine, you're rising with the city, perched atop a penthouse, eyes closed, the world below but a gentle hum. It's not the luxury of the space that captivates every observer, but the ethereal glow that bathes you. That, my darling, is the Manhattan Morning Embrace—an intimate dance with dawn that exudes tranquility, clarity, and an alluring allure all its own.

In this ethereal chapter of The Manhattan Diaries, we'll delve deep into the tranquil terraces that cradle the city's soul. From the gentle inhales that welcome the sun's first rays to the deliberate exhales that dance with the city's awakening, you'll unlock the secret to harmonizing with the metropolis' mosaic of moments.

But this isn't just about breathing in and out—oh no. It's about melding with Manhattan's multifaceted soul, about meditating with a purpose, a vision, an epiphany. It's about understanding the skyscrapers not as mere buildings, but as timeless guardians of dreams, and the shadows they cast as whispers of tales untold.

Join me, as we ascend to the city's zeniths, embrace the hues of the heavens, and master the art of a meditation that doesn't just ground you, but elevates the spirit of the entire city. For here in Manhattan, every sunrise isn't just a new beginning, but a masterpiece in the making. Rise and shine, darling, for the skyline serenades your spirit. Welcome to The Manhattan Diaries— where your meditation can be as magical as the city's dawn duet.

RISE AND SHINE, MANHATTAN STYLE

The Penthouse Oasis: Where Manhattan Dreams Take Flight

In the enchanting world of Manhattan, where life's stories are written against the backdrop of towering skyscrapers, there exists a realm that's a cut above the rest—a realm where dreams ascend to the heavens. Picture it: penthouses, the jewels of this city's crown, where luxury and sophistication intertwine with the very essence of Manhattan's spirit. Join me as we rise to these penthouse retreats, where dreams soar higher than the skyline itself.

➢ **Where Skyline Meets Sanctuary**: Imagine coming home to a space that hovers above the bustling streets of New York, an oasis that's as serene as it is sophisticated. A penthouse isn't just an apartment—it's a statement. It's where you get to say, "I've made it," every time you step into your private domain, where the frenetic energy of Manhattan can be admired from a perfect distance. Here, the city is yours to savor, right from your own panoramic perch.

➢ **Designer Décor with a Side of Edge**: These aren't cookie-cutter interiors, darling. Each penthouse is a crafted masterpiece, adorned with high-end finishes and custom-designed furniture that balances elegance with an unapologetic dash of edginess. Think Italian leather, hand-sculpted pieces, and iconic art framing every corner. There's an energy in these rooms that's unmistakably New York, combining classic luxury with an avant-garde twist. In these spaces, every detail tells its own glamorous story.

➢ **A Glamorous Hideaway**: When it comes to social sanctuaries, penthouses are the epitome of the upper echelon. Imagine escaping from the noise and revelry below, retreating to a space that feels secluded yet inviting. These penthouses are where private cocktail parties and intimate gatherings unfold under the shimmering city lights. Here, the buzz of the world fades, replaced by a curated crowd and a sense of luxury that feels both exclusive and electrifying. It's your private hideaway, tailored for the ultimate insiders.

➤ **Views That Make Your Heart Skip a Beat**: Waking up to a view that sweeps across the skyline and stretches out to iconic landmarks like the Statue of Liberty or Central Park? Only in a penthouse, darling. These sweeping vistas turn your walls into windows to the world, with New York's endless skyline as your daily backdrop. You're not just living with a view; you're living *in* the view, every sunrise and sunset painting the city anew. It's breathtaking, intimate, and uniquely yours.

➤ **A Stroll Away from the City's Elite Hotspots**: Living in the clouds doesn't mean you're disconnected from the vibrancy of Manhattan life. Your penthouse keeps you nestled in the city's elite neighborhoods, mere steps from designer boutiques, Michelin-starred restaurants, and the art galleries that set the world on fire. You're both a part of the city's energy and above it, making each night out as accessible as a walk down a private elevator to a world at your fingertips.

In this whirlwind journey through Manhattan's penthouse paradise, we can't help but be reminded of the city's most iconic landmarks. Think of Central Park, an oasis in the midst of urban chaos, or the Empire State Building, standing tall as a beacon of timeless grandeur. And of course, Lady Liberty, extending her embrace to all who dare to dream. These are the markers of Manhattan's enchantment, the very essence that defines this city of dreams. So, my darlings, embrace the allure of penthouse living, let the sunrise serenades fill your soul, and remember that in this city where even the sky's the limit, the penthouse oasis is where Manhattan's dreams take flight.

Completed Tasks: Sky High Oasis Activities

_____
_____
_____
_____
_____
_____
_____
_____
_____
_____
_____
_____
_____
_____
_____
_____
_____
_____
_____
_____
_____
_____
_____

Inspirational Quote

DECIDE WHAT YOU WANT; DECIDE WHAT YOU ARE WILLING TO EXCHANGE FOR IT. ESTABLISH YOUR PRIORITIES AND GO TO WORK. — H. L. Hunt

PENTHOUSE PERSPECTIVES

Action Items: Intentions and Thoughts

RISE AND SHINE, MANHATTAN STYLE

Sunrise Chronicles: The Love Story Between Manhattan and the Morning Sun

In the glamorous tapestry of Manhattan, where love stories are woven into the very fabric of life, there exists a timeless romance—a love story between the city and the morning sun. Imagine it: the city that never sleeps, awakening each day with a passionate embrace of dawn's first light. Join me as we delve into this enchanting affair, where Manhattan's heart beats in harmony with the sun, and where the sunrise becomes a daily testament to the city's enduring allure.

➤ **A Golden Prelude to the Day**: As the first rays stretch over the skyline, Manhattan awakens in a warm, golden glow, like a lover touched by morning light. The city, wrapped in shadows and mist, begins to reveal itself with an ethereal beauty, setting the tone for another vibrant day.

➤ **Reflections on Glass and Steel**: The sunrise dances across the skyscrapers, casting shimmering reflections on glass and steel. The buildings become a canvas, capturing the sun's colors and transforming the cityscape into a work of art—a fleeting masterpiece that belongs only to those awake to witness it.

➤ **Central Park's Secret Symphony**: At dawn, Central Park breathes a sigh of peace as soft sunlight filters through the trees. The lake mirrors the pastel sky, and the morning mist lingers, creating a tranquil world within the city—a hidden retreat for the early risers who stroll through its pathways.

➤ **Rooftops Bathed in Radiance**: For those who begin their day with coffee on a rooftop, the view is nothing short of magical. The sun's first light washes over terraces, gardens, and balconies, inviting the city's residents to pause and soak in the beauty that surrounds them before the rush begins.

16

PENTHOUSE PERSPECTIVES

- ➢ **A Serenade of Silence**: In these quiet moments, Manhattan's usual hum is replaced by a soft, almost reverent stillness. The streets are empty, the noise subdued, and for a brief time, the city feels like a secret—a private experience shared only by the sun, the city, and those lucky enough to be awake.

- ➢ **A Promise of Possibilities**: Every sunrise is a reminder of Manhattan's limitless spirit. As the day's first light spills over the Hudson, it brings with it a sense of renewal—a gentle reminder that every day in the city holds endless opportunities, waiting to be embraced as fervently as the city embraces the sun.

- ➢ **The River's Morning Glow**: As the sun rises, the Hudson and East Rivers come alive with a soft, golden light. Boats drift lazily on the glowing water, and the bridges cast long shadows, creating a serene, cinematic landscape that feels timeless and new every morning.

- ➢ **A Morning for the Dreamers**: For the artists, writers, and thinkers who find inspiration in the city's dawn, each sunrise is like a muse. The light spills into studio windows, over café tables, and onto the steps of brownstones, as Manhattan offers up its heart to those who see beauty in its every detail.

As we embark on this journey through Manhattan's sunrise chronicles, we can't help but be reminded of the city's most iconic landmarks-Central Park, a verdant oasis amidst the urban chaos; the Empire State Building, a timeless sentinel watching over the city's love story with the sun; and Lady Liberty, forever extending her embrace to all dreamers. These landmarks, like chapters in a grand novel, stand as testaments to Manhattan's enduring allure, where even the sky's the limit. So, my darlings, let the love story between Manhattan and the morning sun inspire you, for in this city where dreams take flight, each sunrise is a masterpiece, a narrative of elegance and timeless romance.

Completed Tasks: Sunrise Chronicles Activities

Inspirational Quote

THE GOLDEN MOMENTS IN THE STREAM OF LIFE RUSH PAST US, AND WE SEE NOTHING BUT SAND; THE ANGELS COME TO VISIT US, AND WE ONLY KNOW THEM WHEN THEY ARE GONE. — George Eliot

18

Action Items: Intentions and Thoughts

Meditation in the Sky: Finding Zen Amidst the Concrete Jungle

In the whirlwind of Manhattan's concrete jungle, amidst the relentless pace of life, there exists a hidden sanctuary—a realm where tranquility and Zen merge with the urban chaos. Picture it: meditation in the sky, a practice that goes beyond the ordinary, a way to find serenity amidst the skyscrapers. Join me as we embark on a journey to unlock the secrets of mindfulness in the heart of Manhattan, where finding Zen isn't just a practice; it's an art form.

> ➤ **Zen with a View**: Imagine meditating with the city sprawled out beneath you, as the sun casts a warm glow across the skyline. You're not just sitting still; you're ascending to a realm where the city's heartbeat syncs with your breath, and every inhale feels like a step closer to heaven.

> ➤ **Designer Serenity**: These sky-high sanctuaries aren't your typical ashrams, darling. Think minimalist elegance with a side of urban glamour—floor-to-ceiling windows, plush meditation cushions, and curated crystals that blend modern chic with ancient calm.

> ➤ **Breathing Above the Chaos**: In a city that never stops, finding calm in the clouds is a triumph. Up here, you can breathe deeply without the city's usual frenzy seeping in, and each breath feels like a decadent luxury, grounding you in a way that only Manhattan's finest heights can.

> ➤ **Luxury Meets Mindfulness**: This isn't just meditation; it's a lifestyle. Picture high-rise yoga studios with ambient lighting, Tibetan sound bowls, and a soundtrack that includes both soft jazz and soothing chants. Because who says Zen can't come with a touch of indulgence?

> ➤ **The Sunrise Ritual**: Nothing says tranquility quite like watching the sunrise while seated in a meditation nook 40 floors above street level.

The sky transforms, your heart rate slows, and for a few precious moments, the city is yours to savor in peaceful stillness.

➤ **Floating Above Reality**: Up here, the noise and hustle feel like a world away. In your sky-high retreat, it's just you and your thoughts—anchored in mindfulness, suspended above the city like you're in your own private nirvana.

➤ **Manhattan's Mindful Elite**: You're in good company, surrounded by a tribe of like-minded souls who know that calm is the ultimate luxury. Together, you're embracing the art of slowing down in a city where fast is the only speed, proving that mindfulness is the ultimate status symbol.

➤ **Zen as an Art Form**: This is Manhattan, where even meditation has a little edge. From sculpted Zen gardens to serene water features, these elevated sanctuaries are more than spaces—they're an experience. Because in the city that sets trends, even finding peace is an art unto itself.

➤ **An Elevated Escape**: Up here, meditation becomes a true escape— a space where Manhattan's buzz fades to a gentle hum, leaving only you, the sky, and a perfect moment of clarity.

As we explore the art of meditation in the sky, it's impossible not to be reminded of Manhattan's most iconic landmarks—Central Park, where nature's serenity flourishes amidst the concrete; the One World Observatory, where you can meditate amidst the clouds; and the Metropolitan Museum of Art, where even the art itself whispers mindfulness. These landmarks serve as beacons of inspiration, reminding us that in this city of constant movement, finding Zen is not just a practice; it's a reflection of Manhattan's soul. So, my darlings, embrace the art of meditation in the sky, let it elevate your spirit, and remember that in Manhattan, amidst the urban jungle, inner peace is not just a possibility—it's a necessity.

Completed Tasks: Finding Zen Activities

_____
_____
_____
_____
_____
_____
_____
_____
_____
_____
_____
_____
_____
_____
_____
_____
_____
_____
_____
_____
_____
_____
_____
_____

Inspirational Quote

I WANT TO LIVE MY LIFE, NOT RECORD IT. — Jackie Kennedy

Action Items: Intentions and Thoughts

_____

_____

_____

_____

_____

_____

_____

_____

_____

_____

_____

_____

_____

_____

_____

_____

_____

_____

_____

_____

_____

_____

_____

_____

_____

_____

_____

_____

Whispers in the Shadows: The Untold Stories of Manhattan's Skyscrapers

In the luminous tapestry of Manhattan, where each skyscraper reaches for the heavens, there lies a world of secrets—a realm where the towering giants harbor untold stories. Picture it: whispers in the shadows, tales that echo through the city's concrete canyons, and histories hidden within their steel frames. Join me as we embark on a journey to unveil the enigmatic narratives of Manhattan's skyscrapers, where these architectural marvels are not just buildings, but timeless guardians of dreams.

- ➤ **The Glamorous Beginnings**: Each skyscraper rose from bold dreams and grand visions. Built on ambition, power, and a touch of scandal, these buildings are more than concrete—they're the ultimate status symbols, each with its own illustrious origin story.

- ➤ **Hidden Haunts of the Elite**: Behind locked doors and private elevators are the exclusive bars, speakeasies, and penthouses where Manhattan's power players cut deals and toast to their successes. It's all very hush-hush, of course, but you know there's a story behind every high-rise soirée.

- ➤ **Architectural Affairs**: Some of these skyscrapers were born from rivalries, with architects vying to outdo each other in height, design, and prestige. Manhattan's skyline is essentially a love letter—and a battle cry—etched in steel and glass.

- ➤ **Ghosts of Deals Past**: The boardrooms and lobbies have seen fortunes made and lost, each one echoing with whispers of bygone moguls, fallen empires, and the deals that shaped the city we know today. Oh, if these walls could talk, the stories they'd spill!

- ➤ **Style Icons in the Sky**: Every skyscraper has a personality. From the sleek minimalism of One World Trade Center to the art deco elegance of the Chrysler Building, these icons embody different eras, reminding us that fashion isn't just for the runway—it's for the skyline, too.

> **Secrets Beneath the Surface**: Many skyscrapers have hidden floors, underground tunnels, or secret staircases leading to nowhere. These elements weren't just architectural quirks; they were built for intrigue, escape, or exclusivity—a touch of mystery for those in the know.

> **The Power of Presence**: Some buildings just have an undeniable energy, as if they're breathing in the city's essence. The Empire State Building, for instance, isn't just a landmark; it's a symbol, standing tall through the city's highs and lows, radiating resilience and glamor.

> **Silent Guardians of Dreams**: At the end of the day, these skyscrapers aren't just buildings—they're the keepers of Manhattan's legacy. They've watched over countless lives, ambitions, and dreams, bearing silent witness to a city that never stops reaching for the stars.

As we unravel the enigmatic narratives of Manhattan's skyscrapers, we can't help but be reminded of the city's most iconic landmarks—Times Square, where the neon lights tell stories of the Broadway stage; the Flatiron Building, standing as a testament to architectural innovation; and the New York Public Library, where history's whispers echo through the hallowed halls. These landmarks serve as anchors in Manhattan's ever-evolving story, reminding us that the skyscrapers are not just towering structures; they're guardians of dreams, silent witnesses to the city's rise and reinvention. So, my darlings, as we delve into the secrets hidden within these shadows, let us embrace the skyscrapers as storytellers of Manhattan's past, present, and future, where every whisper in the shadows is a testament to the city's enduring legacy.

Completed Tasks: Untold Stories Activities

Inspirational Quote

I STILL FIND EACH DAY TOO SHORT FOR ALL THE THOUGHTS I WANT TO THINK, ALL THE WALKS I WANT TO TAKE, ALL THE BOOKS I WANT TO READ, AND ALL THE FRIENDS I WANT TO SEE. — John Burroughs

Action Items: Intentions and Thoughts

The Manhattan Masterpiece: Capturing Dawn's Splendor

In the luminous tapestry of Manhattan, where dreams are painted against the canvas of the cityscape, there exists a daily masterpiece—a moment when the city herself becomes a work of art. Picture it: capturing dawn's splendor, a practice that goes beyond the ordinary, a way to immortalize the enchantment of a Manhattan morning. Join me as we embark on a journey to unlock the secrets of preserving the city's radiant sunrise, where every dawn is not just a new beginning, but a masterpiece in the making.

> ➤ **A Sky Painted in Pastels**: Every sunrise in Manhattan is a new canvas, with shades of pink, lavender, and gold illuminating the skyline like a blush on the city's cheeks. It's nature's own little art show, perfectly curated for those who rise early enough to catch it.

> ➤ **The Morning Glow of Glass and Steel**: As dawn breaks, the skyscrapers catch the light, reflecting hues that turn every high-rise into a glistening jewel. It's as if each building is dressed in its morning best, ready to greet the day with a touch of glamour.

> ➤ **A Central Park Serenade**: Picture yourself strolling through Central Park just as the first light filters through the trees. The lake shimmers, the paths are quiet, and it's just you, Manhattan, and the promise of a new day—a morning symphony played just for you.

> ➤ **Coffee with a Side of Sunrise**: Imagine sipping your morning latte at a rooftop café, the skyline stretching out before you, bathed in the first light of day. There's a decadence in the simplicity—a feeling that this is your private show, and the city's performing just for you.

> ➤ **Rivers Wrapped in Radiance**: As dawn unfolds, the Hudson and East Rivers glow with golden light, casting reflections of the city back into the water. It's a moment where Manhattan seems to be admiring herself, a perfect union of city and sky.

➢ **The Energy of a New Day**: Manhattan at dawn has a palpable energy, a subtle hum that says, "Today is yours." It's a city poised on the edge of greatness, reminding you that every day here holds the potential for something extraordinary.

➢ **The Secret Gardens Awaken**: High above the streets, rooftop gardens and terraces come to life as the sun spills over them. These hidden oases, tucked away atop the city, become lush retreats where morning light adds an air of magic to every leaf and blossom.

➢ **The City's Heartbeat in the Quiet**: For a few precious moments, the city is still, the hum of the day yet to begin. Standing above it all, you can feel Manhattan's heartbeat—a rhythm that pulses with hope, beauty, and the promise of another brilliant day in the city that never stops dreaming.

➢ **A Cinematic Goodbye to the Stars**: As dawn takes hold, the last stars fade from the Manhattan sky, leaving a sense of mystery lingering in the early light. It's like the final scene of a classic film, where the night's secrets gently slip away, making room for the city's next chapter to unfold under a fresh, radiant sky.

As we unravel the secrets of capturing dawn's splendor, it's impossible not to be reminded of Manhattan's most iconic landmarks—The High Line, where urban and natural beauty converge; St. Patrick's Cathedral, where spiritual devotion meets architectural grandeur; and the Museum of Modern Art, where creativity and innovation are celebrated. These landmarks serve as constant sources of inspiration, reminding us that every sunrise in Manhattan is a masterpiece, a testament to the city's enduring allure. So, my darlings, embrace the art of capturing dawn's splendor, let it inspire your creativity, and remember that in Manhattan, where even the sky's the limit, each morning is a fresh opportunity to create your own masterpiece, painted with the colors of dawn.

Completed Tasks: Dawn's Splendor Activities

_____

_____

_____

_____

_____

_____

_____

_____

_____

_____

_____

_____

_____

_____

_____

_____

_____

_____

_____

_____

_____

_____

_____

_____

_____

_____

Inspirational Quote

THE CHIEF DANGER IN LIFE IS THAT YOU MAY TAKE TOO MANY PRECAUTIONS. — Alfred Adler

Action Items: Intentions and Thoughts

Action Items: Intentions and Thoughts

_____

_____

_____

_____

_____

_____

_____

_____

_____

_____

_____

_____

_____

_____

_____

_____

_____

_____

_____

_____

_____

_____

_____

_____

_____

_____

_____

_____

Café Society: The Art of the Manhattan Morning Latte Ritual

Manhattan, a city that doesn't just wake up—it comes alive, pulsating with a vibrant energy that demands your utmost presence. In this jungle of steel and aspirations, it's not just about seizing the day, but how you herald its dawn—with a dash of elegance, a spoonful of spirit, and an aroma that's uniquely you.

Imagine: As dawn paints the city in hues of gold, you're nestled in a corner café off Madison Avenue. Every gaze that drifts towards you isn't aimed at the jewels around your neck, but the mesmerizing dance of steam rising from your latte. That, dear reader, is the Manhattan Morning Ritual, a whispered secret between you and the city, speaking of old-world charm and new-age dreams.

In this intoxicating chapter of The Manhattan Diaries, we'll whisk you away into the world of coffee beans and urban legends. From the gentle cares of a barista's hands, echoing the sultry embrace of the city's morning air, to the fiery passion of a freshly brewed espresso shot, reminiscent of a diva taking center stage—you're about to redefine your morning coffee rendezvous.

Yet, it's more than a beverage—it's liquid art. It's about letting the coffeehouse cacophony serenade your soul, about cradling a cup infused with tales of ambition, love, and fleeting moments. Embrace the café corners, where whispered dreams blend seamlessly with the city's heartbeat.

So, let's embark on this aromatic adventure, discovering nooks where every sip resonates with Manhattan's allure. Because, sweetheart, here in Manhattan, your morning latte isn't just a drink; it's a rite of passage. Brace yourself, the city has brewed an escapade just for you. Welcome to The Manhattan Diaries—where every sunrise ushers in a tale as timeless as your favorite brew.

The Chic Coffeehouses of Manhattan: Where Latte Dreams Come True

In the dazzling labyrinth of Manhattan, where every corner exudes an aura of sophistication and style, lies a treasure trove of chic coffeehouses. Picture it: the hustle and bustle of city life outside, but within, a sanctuary of taste and tranquility awaits. These are the coffeehouses where latte dreams come true, where your morning rendezvous is as much about fashion as it is about flavor. Join me, as we embark on a journey to uncover the chic coffeehouses that define Manhattan's café society, where the art of sipping a latte becomes an art form all its own.

> ➤ **Elegance in Every Cup**: Step into these coffeehouses, and you're met with an ambiance that's all about understated luxury. From marble countertops to artisanal ceramic mugs, every detail is as carefully curated as the espresso itself.

> ➤ **The Perfect People-Watching Perch**: These cafés are prime spots for watching Manhattan's best-dressed stroll by. Park yourself by a window, latte in hand, and soak up the scene as the city's most stylish put on their impromptu runway show just for you.

> ➤ **Latte Art, Elevated**: This isn't just foam; it's art. Think heart-shaped patterns, delicate swirls, and even portraits in the froth—because in Manhattan, even your coffee should make a statement.

> ➤ **Fashionably Flavorful**: These coffeehouses serve flavors as sophisticated as the clientele. Expect hints of lavender, cardamom, and rose in your cup, and pair it with a pastry that's practically couture. A lavender latte with an almond croissant? Divine.

> ➤ **Décor to Die For**: Each coffeehouse is an Instagram dream, designed with exposed brick, vintage chandeliers, and plush seating.

It's the kind of place that feels like a secret—yet everyone in the know is already there.

➢ **A Sanctuary Amidst the Rush**: In the middle of Manhattan's energy, these cafés offer an escape. You slip inside, and it's as if the city's noise melts away, replaced by soft jazz and the gentle hum of conversation—a pocket of peace just for you.

➢ **Meet Me for a "Café Date"**: These are the spots where meetings are made, friends gather, and romances spark. Whether it's a business deal or a blind date, there's no better backdrop than a stylish Manhattan coffeehouse to set the scene.

➢ **An All-Day Affair**: Some of these coffeehouses turn into lounges by night, swapping coffee for cocktails. It's where the espresso martinis flow, and the crowd lingers long after dark, proving that in Manhattan, café culture is truly 24/7 glamour.

➢ **Signature Sips with a Dash of Glamour**: Each coffeehouse has its own iconic drink—think saffron cappuccinos or honey-lavender matchas—making every sip feel like a taste of Manhattan's chicest secrets.

As we savor the chic coffeehouses of Manhattan, it's impossible not to be reminded of the city's most iconic landmarks—the Guggenheim Museum, where art and architecture collide in a whirl of inspiration; Central Park, a sprawling oasis of nature amidst the urban hustle; and the Whitney Museum of American Art, a testament to the city's ever-evolving creative spirit. These landmarks stand as beacons of culture and style, reflecting Manhattan's enduring allure. So, my darlings, let the chic coffeehouses of this vibrant city become your personal sanctuaries, where latte dreams come true and where every sip resonates with the sophistication of Manhattan's artistic soul. Welcome to The Manhattan Diaries, where every sunrise holds a tale as stylish as your favorite brew.

Completed Tasks: Chic Coffeehouse Activities

_____
_____
_____
_____
_____
_____
_____
_____
_____
_____
_____
_____
_____
_____
_____
_____
_____
_____
_____
_____
_____
_____
_____
_____
_____

Inspirational Quote

DO THE DIFFICULT THINGS WHILE THEY ARE EASY AND DO THE GREAT THINGS WHILE THEY ARE SMALL. A JOURNEY OF A THOUSAND MILES MUST BEGIN WITH A SINGLE STEP. — Lao Tzu

Action Items: Intentions and Thoughts

Barista Artistry: The Coffee Connoisseurs Behind the Magic

In the captivating world of Manhattan's chic coffeehouses, where every latte is a work of art, there are unsung heroes—the coffee connoisseurs, the baristas who turn every cup into a masterpiece. Picture it: the aroma of freshly ground beans, the rhythmic hiss of the espresso machine, and the skilled hands that craft each latte with love and precision. Join me, as we venture behind the scenes to discover the barista artistry that elevates Manhattan's coffee culture to new heights, where your morning ritual becomes a canvas for their creative expression.

- ➤ **The True Alchemists of Aroma**: These baristas know their beans inside out, selecting roasts that create the perfect aroma. It's like they're casting a spell with each grind, filling the café with a fragrance that says, "Welcome to your day's first luxury."

- ➤ **Precision in Every Pour**: When they pour, it's a performance. Every movement is intentional, with a finesse that turns simple coffee into high art. From the tilt of the cup to the angle of the pour, it's all about capturing perfection in each swirl.

- ➤ **Latte Art with Personality**: Forget the basic heart design—these baristas go all out. Swans, rosettas, and even abstract designs appear in the foam, making each cup a mini masterpiece that's almost too beautiful to drink. Almost.

- ➤ **Masters of Flavor Fusion**: These coffee connoisseurs aren't just baristas; they're mixologists, infusing unexpected flavors like rose, lavender, and spices into espresso creations that feel tailored to each customer's sophisticated taste.

- ➤ **Crafting the Perfect Froth**: The texture of a latte is everything, and they know it. With milk steamed to silky perfection, the froth is velvety and indulgent, adding an extra layer of luxury to every sip.

➤ **Rituals Rooted in Passion**: Watching these baristas work is like witnessing a passion project. They greet each coffee order as a new opportunity to craft, to create, to connect, making your morning cup feel like an experience, not a transaction.

➤ **Espresso Experts with Style**: They're not only skilled but effortlessly stylish—every bit the Manhattanite with flair. Aprons, rolled sleeves, and a touch of elegance—these baristas don't just serve coffee; they serve it with a side of chic.

➤ **A Secret Society of Coffee Artists**: These baristas share an unspoken bond, a community of artisans who take pride in their craft. It's as if they're part of a secret society, a world of coffee artistry known only to those who step into Manhattan's finest coffeehouses.

➤ **Masters of the Morning Ritual**: These baristas don't just make coffee; they create a morning experience. With every cup, they transform a simple caffeine fix into a cherished ritual, welcoming each customer with warmth and a sense of familiarity that turns the café into your own personal sanctuary.

As we uncover the barista artistry that fuels Manhattan's coffee culture, it's impossible not to be reminded of the city's most iconic landmarks—The Met, Where artistry in every form is celebrated; the Apollo Theater, where creativity and innovation find their stage; and the Gantry Plaza State Park, where the skyline's reflection dances on the East River's surface. So, my darlings, let the coffee connoisseurs behind the magic remind you that in Manhattan, even your morning latte is a form of artistry, an expression of the city's vibrant soul. Welcome to The Manhattan Diaries, where each sunrise is a canvas for inspiration, painted with the flavors of coffee and the hands of skilled baristas.

Completed Tasks: Behind the Magic Activities

Inspirational Quote

ONE WAY TO KEEP MOMENTUM GOING IS TO HAVE CONSTANTLY GREATER GOALS. — Michael Korda

Action Items: Intentions and Thoughts

Manhattan's Signature Latte Creations: Sipping on the City's Flavors

In the heart of Manhattan, where every street corner tells a different story, there exists a delightful realm where coffee becomes a canvas for creativity—the world of signature latte creations. Picture it: the aroma of artisanal beans mingling with the city's hustle and bustle, each sip a taste of Manhattan's diverse flavors and cultures. Join me as we embark on a journey to savor Manhattan's signature latte creations, where coffee becomes a symphony of taste, and each cup reflects the city's vibrant spirit.

- **The Honey-Lavender Dream**: Imagine a latte infused with soft floral notes and a touch of honey's natural sweetness—it's like holding a piece of springtime right in your hands, even if it's the dead of winter. Each sip feels as refreshing as a stroll through Central Park when the flowers are in full bloom.

- **The Maple-Spiced Marvel**: With cinnamon and a hint of maple syrup, this latte captures all the cozy vibes of a crisp fall morning in the city. It's as warming as a cashmere scarf wrapped around your shoulders, a little indulgence that's perfect for those days when you want to sip something that feels as comforting as it is sophisticated.

- **Matcha Meets Manhattan**: This isn't your typical matcha. It's a creamy, vanilla-infused green delight with a boost of energy and a touch of zen. Think of it as the latte for the Manhattanite who needs a kickstart to the day but craves a moment of calm amidst the city's constant hum.

- **Cardamom-Chai Fusion**: A true cosmopolitan twist on the classic chai, this latte combines cardamom's rich spiciness with a velvety, frothy finish. Each sip is like a mini-escape to somewhere exotic, yet it's unmistakably Manhattan in its chic, sophisticated blend.

➢ **Saffron and Rose Gold Latte**: This is luxury in a cup—a delicate dance of saffron and rose that feels like an ode to the city's cultural richness. It's daring, fragrant, and a bit mysterious, like Manhattan itself, offering an experience that's bold yet refined.

➢ **The Hudson Mocha**: Rich dark chocolate meets a pinch of sea salt in this mocha, creating a drink that's as layered and bold as Manhattan's history. Every sip is deeply satisfying, a perfect choice for those who crave a bit of indulgence with flavors that linger long after the last drop.

➢ **The Espresso Tonic Twist**: For the daring and adventurous, this espresso tonic combines smooth espresso with bubbly tonic water and a splash of citrus. It's the perfect daytime refresher, an energizing blend that's as bold and unexpected as a walk down Fifth Avenue.

➢ **The Golden Turmeric Latte**: Spiced to perfection with a sprinkle of cinnamon on top, this golden latte is both trendy and timeless. It's like sipping the golden glow of a Manhattan sunset, warming you from the inside out with each luxurious, earthy sip.

As we savor Manhattan's signature latte creations, it's impossible not to be reminded of the city's most iconic landmarks—The Museum of Modern Art, where creativity knows no bounds; the Chrysler Building, an architectural masterpiece that captures the city's elegance; and Grand Central Terminal, the bustling heart of Manhattan's transportation hub. These landmarks stand as symbols of the city's enduring creativity, artistry, and dynamism, much like the signature lattes that celebrate Manhattan's diverse flavors. So, my darlings, let these lattes be your passports to the city's culinary tapestry, where each sip takes you on a journey through Manhattan's vibrant neighborhoods and iconic landmarks. Welcome to The Manhattan Diaries, where every sunrise is a taste of the city's soul.

Completed Tasks: Signature Lattes Activities

Inspirational Quote

THE WILL TO WIN, THE DESIRE TO SUCCEED, THE URGE TO REACH YOUR FULL POTENTIAL . . . THESE ARE THE KEYS THAT WILL UNLOCK THE DOOR TO PERSONAL EXCELLENCE. — Confucius

CAFÉ SOCIETY

Action Items: Intentions and Thoughts

RISE AND SHINE, MANHATTAN STYLE

Latte as a Lifestyle: The Power of the Morning Ritual

In the grand tapestry of Manhattan's daily rhythm, the morning latte isn't just a beverage; it's a lifestyle choice, a powerful ritual that sets the tone for the day. Picture it: the city's early risers, poised in coffeehouses like modern-day explorers, crafting their morning moments with precision. Join me as we delve into the power of the morning latte ritual, where coffee isn't just a drink—it's a declaration of intent, a statement of readiness to conquer the city that never sleeps.

- ➢ **A Touch of Glamour in Every Sip**: The morning latte isn't just a coffee; it's your first accessory of the day. A Honey-Lavender Dream is like putting on a splash of perfume—subtle, yet powerful—an elegant detail that sets the mood for whatever the city has in store.

- ➢ **A Springtime Escape in Winter's Chill**: This latte is pure poetry for the senses. With its delicate floral notes, each sip transports you to a spring day in Central Park, even when Manhattan's winter winds are blowing. It's a private escape wrapped in warmth.

- ➢ **Refinement with a Twist**: Honey-lavender isn't just a flavor; it's a statement of taste. This latte whispers sophistication, offering a perfect balance of floral and sweet that's as unexpected as it is delightful—an indulgence that feels effortlessly chic.

- ➢ **Crafted for the Connoisseur**: This isn't just a coffee for the caffeine rush. The Honey-Lavender Dream is curated for those who appreciate the artistry in their latte, a drink crafted with love and precision, like a piece of fine art in every cup.

- ➢ **A Ritual of Rejuvenation**: Each sip of this latte feels like a mini refresh. The honey soothes, the lavender calms, and suddenly, you're not just drinking coffee; you're setting a peaceful, positive tone for the day—a moment to savor before the city's hustle begins.

➤ **An Insider's Secret**: Not everyone knows the magic of a honey-lavender latte. It's a drink that feels like a little secret between you and the barista, a quiet nod to those who know the finer things in life.

➤ **Elevating the Everyday**: With its elegant blend of flavors, the Honey-Lavender Dream transforms the simple act of grabbing coffee into a morning ritual. It's an experience, a moment of beauty in the everyday routine—perfect for the Manhattanite who savors the details.

➤ **Your Morning Mantra in a Cup**: This isn't just a coffee; it's your daily declaration. As you sip, you're making a promise to the day: to embrace elegance, to be present, and to face the city's challenges with calm confidence. It's your statement of readiness, one delicious sip at a time.

➤ **A Floral Escape in a Cup**: The Honey-Lavender Dream brings a touch of nature to the city's morning rush—a little bouquet in every sip, reminding you that there's always room for beauty amidst.

As we immerse ourselves in the power of the morning latte ritual, it's impossible not to be reminded of the city's most iconic landmarks—Times Square, where the world gathers to celebrate the arts and entertainment; the Statue of Liberty, a symbol of freedom and opportunity; and the High Line, where nature and urbanity coexist in harmony. These landmarks embody the spirit of Manhattan, where ambition meets opportunity, and where the morning latte is more than a ritual—it's a declaration of readiness to seize the day. So, my darlings, let your morning latte be your daily affirmation, your reminder that in Manhattan, every sunrise is an opportunity, painted with the flavors of coffee and the promise of new beginnings. Welcome to The Manhattan Diaries, where every daybreak holds a tale as powerful as your favorite brew.

Completed Tasks: Morning Latte Ritual Activities

_____

_____

_____

_____

_____

_____

_____

_____

_____

_____

_____

_____

_____

_____

_____

_____

_____

_____

_____

_____

_____

_____

_____

_____

Inspirational Quote

SETTING GOALS IS THE FIRST STEP IN TURNING THE INVISIBLE INTO THE VISIBLE. — Tony Robbins

Action Items: Intentions and Thoughts

Coffeehouse Conversations: Tales Over Latte and Croissants

In the captivating enclaves of Manhattan's coffeehouses, where every latte sip is accompanied by the symphony of chatter and laughter, there exists a unique form of storytelling—a world of coffeehouse conversations. Picture it: the shared tales, the whispered confidences, and the connections that weave the fabric of the city's stories. Join me as we step into the realm of coffeehouse conversations, where lattes and croissants are the backdrop to Manhattan's most intimate narratives, where friendships are forged, romances kindled, and dreams shared over cups of steaming latte.

- ➤ **The Art of the Latte Date**: Manhattanites don't just meet over coffee; they curate a scene. A latte date is a chance to show off a fabulous coat, exchange knowing glances, and let a simple cappuccino turn into an unforgettable encounter.

- ➤ **The Secrets Swirling in Every Sip**: These coffeehouses are like confessionals. From business deals whispered over croissants to love confessions murmured over foam, every table has its story—and each sip feels like you're in on the secret.

- ➤ **Friendships Forged with Foam**: Coffeehouses are the birthplace of friendships that feel like family. Here, lattes are shared, laughter flows, and bonds are formed, proving that some of the city's most enduring relationships are brewed over coffee.

- ➤ **Romance in the Air**: There's something undeniably romantic about a Manhattan café. Couples steal glances across tables, hands reach over to brush a stray crumb, and lattes become love potions, bringing hearts closer with every sip.

- ➤ **The Power Breakfast Club**: Coffeehouses are where Manhattan's movers and shakers gather in the morning, discussing ideas and striking deals over espressos and pain au chocolat. It's the city's most exclusive office—a chic meeting room where caffeine meets ambition.

➢ **A Haven for Dreamers**: Among the chitchat and clinking cups, there's always someone sketching, writing, or daydreaming. These cafés are sanctuaries for the creatives, where ideas are born and passions ignited over a perfect cup.

➢ **The Weekend Ritual**: Coffeehouse conversations reach a whole new level on the weekends. The energy is more relaxed, friends linger longer, and the stories are richer, proving that in Manhattan, Saturdays are for coffee, croissants, and catching up.

➢ **Every Cup Holds a Story**: Each latte or croissant is part of a story, part of the fabric of the city. From the regulars who know each other's orders by heart to the travelers soaking in Manhattan's vibe, coffeehouses are where every Manhattan tale begins.

➢ **The Quiet Bond of Regulars**: Every coffeehouse has its circle of regulars—a knowing nod, a familiar smile, and the shared joy of a perfect latte, creating an unspoken community in the heart of Manhattan.

As we immerse ourselves in the world of coffeehouse conversations, it's impossible not to be reminded of the city's most iconic landmarks—The Strand Bookstore, where literature is celebrated; The Cloisters, a serene oasis in Upper Manhattan; and the 9/11 Memorial, a solemn reminder of the city's resilience. These landmarks stand as witnesses to the stories of Manhattan, where connections are forged, friendships bloom, and dreams are shared. So, my darlings, let these coffeehouse conversations be your reminder that in Manhattan, even over a latte, every moment is a chance for a new story to unfold, a connection to be made, and a memory to be cherished. Welcome to The Manhattan Diaries, where every sunrise holds a tale as intimate as the conversations shared over your favorite brew.

Completed Tasks: Coffeehouse Conversation Activities

_____
_____
_____
_____
_____
_____
_____
_____
_____
_____
_____
_____
_____
_____
_____
_____
_____
_____
_____
_____
_____
_____
_____

Inspirational Quote

YOU ARE NEVER TOO OLD TO SET ANOTHER GOAL OR TO DREAM A NEW DREAM. — Les Brown

CAFÉ SOCIETY

Action Items: Intentions and Thoughts

Action Items: Intentions and Thoughts

_____
_____
_____
_____
_____
_____
_____
_____
_____
_____
_____
_____
_____
_____
_____
_____
_____
_____
_____
_____
_____
_____
_____
_____
_____
_____
_____
_____

The Silk Robe Affair: Embracing Morning Glamour, Room with a View

Manhattan, a city that doesn't just welcome the day—it seduces it with an allure only matched by its own skyline. In a metropolis brimming with movers and shakers, it's not just about greeting the morning, but how you do it—with an elegance that is effortlessly glamorous, yet intimately personal.

Imagine this: You're standing by your floor-to-ceiling windows on the Upper East Side, the cityscape sprawled beneath you. Every sunbeam that filters in doesn't merely glance off the sheen of your silk robe; it dances, celebrating the radiant figure within. That, darling, is the Manhattan Morning Mystique a moment that whispers of private luxuries and audacious dreams, all from the sanctuary of one's own abode.

In this opulent chapter of The Manhattan Diaries, we delve into the intimate affair of embracing morning glamour. From the gentle rustle of silk against skin, reminiscent of secret trysts and whispered love letters, to the bold statement of a sash tied with intent—here lies the magic of starting the day as the diva you truly are.

But remember, it's more than fabric—it's a feeling. It's about sipping that morning coffee with the city at your feet, about letting the early light kiss your skin as it does the towering skyscrapers, understanding the whispered secrets between the two. It's basking in the juxtaposition of soft silk and the city's hard edges.

So, accompany me as we explore the allure of morning rituals that don't just awaken the body, but stir the very soul of Manhattan within you. Because, sweetheart, when you embrace the morning draped in silk, you're not just getting ready for the day—you're setting the stage for an epic. Welcome to The Manhattan Diaries—where dawn's first light reveals not just the city, but the enchantress within.

Dressing for the Manhattan Sunrise: Silk Robes and Morning Glamour

In the shimmering realm of Manhattan's morning rituals, there exists a secret affair with dawn—an art form woven with silk robes and morning glamour. Picture it: the city's early risers, poised by their windows, embracing the sunrise with a grace that's both intimate and utterly glamorous. Join me as we delve into the enchanting world of dressing for the Manhattan sunrise, where silk robes become the canvases for dawn's allure, and every morning is a stage for elegance.

➤ **Silk as a Second Skin**: Nothing says morning luxury like slipping into a silk robe that drapes just so. It's soft, elegant, and moves with a whisper, wrapping you in pure indulgence as you greet the day.

➤ **The Ultimate Accessory: Sunlight**: As dawn's first light pours through the windows, it catches every fold of silk, creating a soft, ethereal glow. In Manhattan, sunlight isn't just lighting—it's your best accessory.

➤ **Effortless Elegance**: Manhattanites know that morning style is all about ease. A chic robe, tousled hair, and a hint of yesterday's perfume lingering on your wrist—there's beauty in looking like you've woken up effortlessly fabulous.

➤ **The Coffee and Couture Combo**: Pairing your morning latte with a silk robe is pure Manhattan chic. Sipping coffee, wrapped in silk, while the city wakes up below? It's a scene that's as iconic as it is indulgent.

➤ **Barely-There Makeup for Maximum Impact**: A touch of tinted moisturizer, a hint of lip balm, and just a dab of highlighter—morning glamour is all about that natural glow, a look that says, "Yes, I woke up like this."

➤ **Statement Robes as Art**: Manhattan's finest know that a robe can be just as much of a statement as an evening gown. Think bold patterns, luxurious fabrics, and elegant cuts that turn your morning routine into a mini fashion moment.

➤ **Dancing in the Dawn**: With the city still quiet, there's something magical about moving through your space as the first light hits. Silk flowing, a little music playing, and the day stretching out before you—it's like your own private dance with the city.

➤ **Elegance Meets Intention**: Dressing up for sunrise isn't just about looking good; it's about setting a tone for the day. In silk and sunlight, you're not just greeting the morning—you're stepping into it with poise, grace, and that unmistakable Manhattan flair.

➤ **A Ritual of Reflection**: Manhattan's early risers take a moment, wrapped in silk, to watch the city stir to life. It's a quiet pause, a breath before the bustle, where elegance meets mindfulness—a reminder that even in the city that never sleeps, there's beauty in the stillness of dawn.

As we immerse ourselves in the world of dressing for the Manhattan sunrise, it's impossible not to be reminded of the city's most iconic landmarks—The Metropolitan Museum of Art, where elegance meets artistry; The Frick Collection, a haven of sophistication; and The Dakota Building, an architectural masterpiece. These landmarks embody the essence of Manhattan's morning glamour, where every daybreak is a canvas for elegance and allure. So, my darlings, let your morning attire be your daily affirmation, your reminder that in Manhattan, every sunrise is an opportunity to embrace the day with grace and glamour. Welcome to The Manhattan Diaries, where each sunrise is an ode to the enchanting world of silk robes and morning splendor.

Completed Tasks: Morning Glamour Activities

_____

_____

_____

_____

_____

_____

_____

_____

_____

_____

_____

_____

_____

_____

_____

_____

_____

_____

_____

_____

_____

_____

_____

_____

_____

Inspirational Quote

ACCEPT THE CHALLENGES SO THAT YOU CAN FEEL THE EXHILARATION OF VICTORY. — George S. Patton

Action Items: Intentions and Thoughts

Upper East Side Elegance: Room with a View and Morning Rituals

In the opulent tapestry of Manhattan's Upper East Side, where grandeur meets refinement, there exists a realm of morning rituals that are nothing short of spectacular—an art of elegance, a room with a view, and an embrace of dawn's enchantment. Picture it: the city's elite, poised by their floor-to-ceiling windows, savoring the sunrise in a manner that's both regal and utterly personal. Join me as we step into the world of Upper East Side elegance, where the morning is greeted from a vantage point of luxury, and every dawn is a symphony of refinement.

➤ **Champagne Sunrises**: The Upper East Side knows how to welcome a new day—with a flute of sparkling water or, for the truly decadent, a touch of champagne as they watch the city wake up beneath them.

➤ **Floor-to-Ceiling Perfection**: Nothing says Upper East Side like panoramic windows that frame the Manhattan skyline. Each morning, these windows are like private paintings, showing dawn's masterpiece in real time.

➤ **Designer Robes Only**: Up here, morning attire is as curated as an evening ensemble. Silk and cashmere robes by La Perla or Loro Piana set the tone, proving that elegance starts from the first layer.

➤ **A Symphony of Silence**: The Upper East Side's mornings are serene and unhurried, with only the faint hum of the city below. It's a moment of pure stillness, a rare and cherished luxury that grounds you before the day's chaos.

➤ **Morning Coffee, Perfected**: Up here, coffee is an art form, served in fine bone china with just the right pour. Sipping espresso as the sunlight spills across the marble countertop is simply part of the ritual.

➤ **The Power of a Signature Scent**: The elite greet the morning with a spritz of their signature fragrance—something timeless and alluring. It's an invisible accessory that lingers, filling the room with a personal touch of luxury.

➤ **Refined Reflections**: Mornings on the Upper East Side are a time for calm reflection, often accompanied by a leather-bound journal or an inspiring novel. It's a mindful pause that combines elegance with intellect, setting the day's intention.

➤ **A Private Audience with the City**: From their high-rise vantage point, Upper East Siders have an exclusive view of Manhattan's beauty as it awakens. It's a reminder that elegance isn't just a look— it's a lifestyle, one that begins with every breathtaking sunrise over the city.

➤ **Morning Jazz Melodies**: The day begins with soft jazz—Miles Davis or Ella Fitzgerald drifting through the room, setting a serene, timeless tone for the Upper East Side morning.

As we bask in the splendor of Upper East Side elegance and morning rituals, it's impossible not to be reminded of the city's most iconic landmarks—The Metropolitan Museum of Art, where elegance meets artistry; Central Park, the urban oasis of tranquility and greenery; and The Frick Collection, a testament to timeless refinement. These landmarks stand as echoes of the Upper East Side's spirit, where grandeur and culture converge in a harmonious embrace. So, my darlings, let the Upper East Side be your inspiration to greet each morning with grace, refinement, and a view that's nothing short of spectacular. Welcome to The Manhattan Diaries, where every sunrise is a testament to the elegance that defines this iconic neighborhood, where the city's heart meets its most splendid form.

Completed Tasks: View Ritual Activities

Inspirational Quote

BELIEVE IN YOURSELF! HAVE FAITH IN YOUR ABILITIES! WITHOUT A HUMBLE BUT REASONABLE CONFIDENCE IN YOUR OWN POWERS, YOU CANNOT BE SUCCESSFUL OR HAPPY. — Norman Vincent Peale

Action Items: Intentions and Thoughts

Whispers of Silk: The Intimate Romance of Morning Rituals

In the quiet hours of Manhattan's dawn, there exists a world of intimate rituals—a delicate dance with morning that's woven with whispers of silk. Picture it: the city's dreamers, wrapped in silk robes, embracing the soft caress of fabric against skin as they welcome the new day. Join me as we step into the realm of whispers of silk, where morning rituals become an intimate romance, a tale of audacious dreams and clandestine trysts, all beneath the gentle light of dawn.

> ➤ **The Caress of Silk**: Sliding into a silk robe as the first light filters in is like slipping into a lover's embrace—soft, delicate, and utterly luxurious. It's a ritual that whispers, "This day is yours."

> ➤ **Barefoot on Marble**: There's something seductive about bare feet on cool marble in the early hours. Each step is a reminder of the quiet power in softness, a delicate balance between strength and grace.

> ➤ **A Mirror Moment**: Standing before the mirror in silk, with dawn casting a soft glow, is a moment of self-reflection that feels both intimate and audacious—a little love note to yourself before the day begins.

> ➤ **The Sensual Sip**: Morning coffee or tea becomes a sensual ritual—held close, savored slowly, with steam mingling with the gentle fabric of silk. It's a taste of elegance, a moment to breathe, a pause before the world awakens.

> ➤ **Perfume and Promise**: A spritz of fragrance on bare skin, just beneath the silk, is like a private secret—an invisible adornment that lingers close, preparing you for the day's mysteries and possibilities.

➢ **The Dance of the Robe**: Silk has a way of moving with you, like a gentle partner in the morning's quiet dance. Each turn, each stretch feels like a delicate choreography, performed just for the morning light.

➢ **Writing Dreams in Ink**: With a journal and pen in hand, morning becomes a time to scribble down dreams, ideas, and private thoughts. It's a ritual that feels like a clandestine tryst with your innermost self—a moment of honesty in the calm before the city's rush.

➢ **A Glance at the World Beyond**: Standing by the window, wrapped in silk, gazing at the city's unfolding day feels like a romance between you and Manhattan itself—a quiet, powerful connection that only dawn and dreams can offer.

➢ **The Soft Serenade of Morning Jazz**: With soft jazz playing faintly in the background, the morning fills with a gentle melody, each note mingling with the silk and the stillness. It's like a private serenade, adding a touch of timeless romance to the dawn's quiet elegance.

As we immerse ourselves in the world of whispers of silk and morning intimacy, it's impossible not to be reminded of the city's most iconic landmarks—The Bethesda Terrace in Central Park, where romance blossoms; The Gramercy Park Hotel, a haven for lovers; and The Rainbow Room, where dreams are celebrated in style. These landmarks are witnesses to Manhattan's most intimate stories, where silk and the city's heartbeat intertwine in harmonious unity. So, my darlings, let your morning rituals be a celebration of intimacy, a reminder that in Manhattan, every sunrise holds the promise of audacious dreams and whispers of romance. Welcome to The Manhattan Diaries, where each morning is an ode to the delicate dance of silk and the tender secrets it holds, a tale as captivating as the city itself.

Completed Tasks: Romance Morning Activities

_____

_____

_____

_____

_____

_____

_____

_____

_____

_____

_____

_____

_____

_____

_____

_____

_____

_____

_____

_____

_____

_____

_____

_____

_____

_____

_____

_____

_____

_____

Inspirational Quote

DON'T THINK, JUST DO. — Horace

Action Items: Intentions and Thoughts

The Manhattan Morning Mystique: Coffee, Silk, and Skyscrapers

In the city that never sleeps, there exists a morning ritual—an affair so enchanting that it seduces the very essence of dawn itself. Picture it: Manhattan's early risers, draped in silk, gazing at the city's skyline from their high-rise windows, savoring the rich aroma of coffee. Join me as we immerse ourselves in The Manhattan Morning Mystique, where coffee, silk, and skyscrapers converge to create a symphony of luxury and allure.

> ➢ **The View from the Top**: There's nothing like sipping coffee from a high-rise window, watching Manhattan come alive below. The city stretches out like your own private kingdom, every skyscraper reflecting the dawn's first light just for you.

> ➢ **The Perfectly Curated Brew**: Manhattan mornings deserve a coffee as refined as the city itself. Whether it's a classic espresso or an exotic blend, each sip is a decadent ritual, as smooth and satisfying as silk against the skin.

> ➢ **A Moment of Velvet Silence**: Before the city's buzz begins, there's a brief, velvet silence in the air. Standing in this stillness, wrapped in silk, feels like a luxurious pause in time—a private, indulgent breath before the day's demands.

> ➢ **The Soft Glow of Sunrise**: The early light paints your space in shades of gold and pink, turning your high-rise into an artful retreat. The glow reflects on your silk robe, adding a soft shimmer that makes every morning feel like a scene from a classic film.

> ➢ **Coffee as an Accessory**: In Manhattan, coffee isn't just a drink— it's a style choice. A steaming cup in hand completes the look, adding a touch of sophistication to the ensemble of silk, skyscrapers, and serene sunrise views.

➢ **A Symphony of Textures**: The smoothness of silk, the warmth of coffee, the coolness of glass—each texture creates a sensory experience that makes the morning feel richer, more layered, a tactile embrace of luxury.

➢ **Journaling with a View**: With Manhattan laid out before you, a journal becomes an essential morning accessory. Thoughts flow as effortlessly as the city's skyline, capturing ideas, dreams, and intentions with the beauty of Manhattan as your muse.

➢ **The Quiet Power of Presence**: In the heart of the city, wrapped in silk and sipping coffee, there's a quiet power in simply being. It's a subtle reminder that in Manhattan, elegance and strength go hand in hand—and every sunrise is an invitation to embody both.

➢ **The Art of Stillness in the City That Moves**: As Manhattan hums awake below, there's a rare tranquility in savoring a quiet moment above it all. Wrapped in silk, coffee in hand, you embrace a stillness that feels almost rebellious—a graceful pause in a city driven by speed.

As we savor The Manhattan Morning Mystique, it's impossible not to be reminded of the city's most iconic landmarks—The Empire State Building, where dreams touch the sky; The High Line, a lush escape above the streets; and One World Trade Center, a testament to resilience and ambition. These landmarks stand as witnesses to the mystique of Manhattan's mornings, where coffee, silk, and skyscrapers create a tapestry of elegance and allure. So, my darlings, let this morning ritual be your daily affirmation, a reminder that in Manhattan, every sunrise is an opportunity to embrace the city's grandeur and make your own mark on the world. Welcome to The Manhattan Diaries, where each dawn unfolds not just the city but the enchantress within.

Completed Tasks: Morning Mystique Activities

_____

_____

_____

_____

_____

_____

_____

_____

_____

_____

_____

_____

_____

_____

_____

_____

_____

_____

_____

_____

_____

_____

_____

_____

_____

_____

Inspirational Quote

GO FOR IT NOW. THE FUTURE IS PROMISED TO NO ONE. — Wayne Dyer

Action Items: Intentions and Thoughts

Action Items: Intentions and Thoughts

_____

_____

_____

_____

_____

_____

_____

_____

_____

_____

_____

_____

_____

_____

_____

_____

_____

_____

_____

_____

_____

_____

_____

_____

_____

Manhattan Mantras:
Uplifting Affirmations for City Divas

Manhattan, a city that doesn't just hum with life—it vibrates with the passion and fervor of a million dreams. Here, amidst the towering facades and roaring avenues, it isn't simply about navigating life's twists and turns; it's about doing it with conviction, allure, and an unmistakable flair.

Picture this: You're perched atop the steps of the Metropolitan Museum, not simply observing the passerby, but absorbing the myriad energies, the hopes and heartbreaks. Each inhale brings the city's essence, each exhale radiates a confidence. That, my love, is the Manhattan Mantra—a whispered affirmation that grounds the spirit and lifts the soul, even amidst the city's chaos.

In this mesmerizing chapter of The Manhattan Diaries, we dive deep into these powerful affirmations. From the introspective reflections whispered during a candle-lit bath to the bold proclamations declared atop rooftop bars, you'll learn the art of crafting mantras that resonate with the rhythm of your heart and the pulse of the city.

But, let's be clear—it's not just about words. It's about forging an inner dialogue, a conversation with the city and oneself. It's about feeling the connection between the self and the sprawling metropolis, realizing that as vast as Manhattan is, your potential is limitless.

Come along, as we navigate the hallowed streets and hidden alleyways, seeking out the perfect affirmations that don't just inspire, but empower. Because, darling, in Manhattan, every thought is an opportunity to redefine yourself. Ready yourself for a transformation, for Manhattan isn't just a backdrop—it's a catalyst. Welcome to The Manhattan Diaries—where your inner voice can echo louder than the city's resounding hustle.

Elevating Your Daily Mantra: Crafting Affirmations for Success

In the relentless rhythm of Manhattan, success is not merely a goal—it's a way of life, an artistry of ambition painted across the city's canvas. Picture it: the city's go-getters, sipping coffee on Park Avenue, crafting affirmations that breathe life into their aspirations. Join me as we ascend the ladder of "Elevating Your Daily Mantra," where affirmations become the foundation of success, each word a brushstroke on the masterpiece of your dreams.

- ➤ **Affirmations as Morning Glamour**: Like slipping into a designer outfit, your affirmation sets the tone for the day. Choose words that radiate confidence, style, and purpose, wrapping you in the elegance of self-assurance.

- ➤ **The Power of "I Am"**: Start with "I am" to claim your identity boldly. Say it with conviction—whether it's "I am unstoppable" or "I am a visionary"—and watch as each word becomes a building block in your empire of dreams.

- ➤ **Channeling the City's Energy**: Let your affirmations mirror Manhattan's hustle and resilience. Words like "limitless" and "unstoppable" give you that edge, grounding you in the city's powerful energy and reminding you that ambition knows no bounds.

- ➤ **Designing Your Success Blueprint**: Affirmations are more than words; they're your blueprint for success. Frame each one with clear intentions like, "I attract opportunities" or "I achieve with ease." Let these phrases guide your every move.

- ➤ **A Daily Power Ritual**: Saying your affirmations is as essential as your morning coffee—a boost for the soul. Recite them as you sip that first cup, infusing your morning ritual with purpose, vision, and drive.

- ➢ **Visualize with Each Word**: Feel each affirmation as though it's already true. See yourself closing deals, seizing opportunities, and conquering challenges. The more vividly you picture it, the closer you get to making it real.

- ➢ **Elegance in Simplicity**: Craft affirmations that are concise yet powerful. Manhattan's elite knows the strength of saying just enough; keep your mantras sharp and impactful, like "I am a magnet for success."

- ➢ **Turn Doubts into Affirmations**: Identify any self-doubt and flip it into an affirmation. Replace "I'm not ready" with "I am prepared," transforming challenges into stepping stones, and building the foundation for a limitless day.

- ➢ **Reflecting in the City's Glow**: Take a moment each evening to revisit your affirmations, letting them resonate as you gaze at the city lights. In Manhattan's glow, affirmations become promises to yourself—a reminder that tomorrow is another chance to elevate, achieve, and thrive.

As we embark on the journey of crafting affirmations for success, it's impossible not to be reminded of the city's most iconic landmarks—The Chrysler Building, where ambition touches the sky; Wall Street, the financial epicenter of the world; and The New York Public Library, a testament to knowledge and inspiration. These landmarks stand as symbols of Manhattan's relentless pursuit of success, where every corner holds the potential to shape your destiny. So, my darlings, let your daily mantra be your compass, guiding you through the labyrinth of ambition and aspirations. Welcome to The Manhattan Diaries, where every affirmation whispered amidst the city's hustle is a brushstroke on the masterpiece of your success, an ode to the spirit of Manhattan that never stops dreaming.

Completed Tasks: Affirmations for Success Activities

_____
_____
_____
_____
_____
_____
_____
_____
_____
_____
_____
_____
_____
_____
_____
_____
_____
_____
_____
_____
_____
_____
_____
_____
_____
_____

Inspirational Quote

THE HARDSHIPS THAT I ENCOUNTERED IN THE PAST WILL HELP ME SUCCEED IN THE FUTURE. — Philip Emeagwali

Action Items: Intentions and Thoughts

Manhattan Moments: Affirmations for Embracing Life's Twists and Turns

In the whirlwind of Manhattan, life unfolds like a captivating drama, filled with unexpected twists and turns. Here, every street corner is a stage, and every moment a chance for reinvention. Picture it: at the heart of Times Square, you're crafting affirmations that breathe resilience into your spirit. Join me as we delve into "Manhattan Moments," where affirmations become your steadfast companions, guiding you through the city's labyrinth of experiences, embracing every twist and turn as part of your unique Manhattan story.

➢ **"I Embrace Change with Elegance"**: In Manhattan, change is the only constant. This affirmation reminds you to flow gracefully through life's shifts, adapting with poise no matter what the city throws your way.

➢ **"I Thrive in the Unexpected"**: The city is full of surprises, and so are you. Embrace every unforeseen moment as a thrilling plot twist in your personal narrative, knowing that you're built for this.

➢ **"Every Setback Fuels My Comeback"**: In the city that never sleeps, resilience is a must. With this affirmation, you're empowered to bounce back stronger after every setback, turning challenges into fuel for your next big move.

➢ **"I Am Unstoppable, Even in Chaos"**: Manhattan's pace can be relentless, but you are even more relentless. This affirmation grounds you in the strength to stay centered and move forward, no matter how chaotic things get.

➢ **"I Create My Own Path"**: Amid the city's bustling crowds and towering skyscrapers, this affirmation reminds you that your journey is uniquely yours. You're not just following a path—you're blazing your own trail.

➤ **"I See Opportunity in Every Corner"**: From Wall Street to SoHo, opportunity is around every corner if you know where to look. Use this affirmation to stay open and receptive, ready to seize the magic in unexpected places.

➤ **"I Am Bold, Fearless, and Ready"**: In Manhattan, boldness is a lifestyle. Embrace this mantra, stepping out each day with a fearless heart, ready for the city's adventures and all its unpredictable beauty.

➤ **"I Am Always Reinventing"**: Reinvention is the essence of Manhattan. This affirmation celebrates your ability to transform, adapt, and evolve—because in this city, every day is an opportunity to redefine who you are.

➤ **"I Find Beauty in Every Moment"**: Manhattan is a city of contrasts, and each one holds its own charm. This affirmation reminds you to pause, breathe, and appreciate the beauty in every experience, whether grand or subtle, as your story unfolds.

As we embrace "Manhattan Moments" and the affirmations that guide us through life's twists and turns, it's impossible not to be reminded of the city's most iconic landmarks—The Flatiron Building, an emblem of resilience; The Brooklyn Bridge, a testament to bridging divides; and Grand Central Terminal, where journeys begin anew. These landmarks stand as witnesses to the city's enduring spirit, where every twist and turn is met with determination and grace. So, my darlings, let your affirmations be the threads that weave the tapestry of your Manhattan story, embracing every moment as part of your unique journey. Welcome to The Manhattan Diaries, where every affirmation whispered amidst the city's drama becomes a testament to your resilience, an ode to the spirit of Manhattan that never stops reinventing itself.

Completed Tasks: Embracing Life's Twists Activities

Inspirational Quote

TO BEGIN, BEGIN. — William Wordsworth

Action Items: Intentions and Thoughts

Inner Dialogue in the City That Never Sleeps: Conversations with Self and Manhattan

In the city that never sleeps, amidst the symphony of sirens and neon lights, there exists an intimate dialogue—an ongoing conversation between self and the metropolis. Picture it: you, standing on the Brooklyn Bridge, gazing at the skyline, engaging in whispered exchanges with Manhattan's soul. Join me as we unravel "Inner Dialogue in the City That Never Sleeps," where conversations with self and Manhattan become the fuel that ignites your dreams and ambitions.

> ➢ **"What's Next?"**: Standing amidst Manhattan's endless energy, you can't help but ask yourself, "What's next?" The city's pulse pushes you forward, daring you to reach higher, to dream bigger, and to chase what's just out of reach.

> ➢ **"I Am One with the City"**: Manhattan's rhythm is intoxicating. In a quiet moment on Fifth Avenue or overlooking the skyline, you feel a seamless connection, a sense that you and the city are part of the same unstoppable force.

> ➢ **"Embrace the Unexpected"**: Manhattan teaches you to welcome surprises, to find beauty in the unexpected twists. In your dialogue, there's an understanding that every detour holds a lesson and every surprise is a part of your story.

> ➢ **"Stay Grounded, Stay Bold"**: With the city as your witness, you remind yourself to keep your feet on the ground, even as your dreams soar. Manhattan's skyscrapers inspire you to rise while staying rooted in who you are.

> ➢ **"The Power Lies Within"**: Manhattan reminds you that true strength doesn't come from the city's glitz but from within. As you

navigate its streets, you feel the inner power that propels you through challenges with unshakable confidence.

➤ **"I Am Part of Something Bigger"**: Looking out at the skyline, you feel a deep sense of belonging. Manhattan whispers that you're part of a grander story, a place where millions chase their dreams, and you're a vital part of that thrilling tapestry.

➤ **"Find the Magic in the Mundane"**: Manhattan's magic lies in its contrasts, in ordinary moments that feel extraordinary. You remind yourself to savor each step, each coffee, each glance—a reminder that beauty lives in the details.

➤ **"I Am Limitless"**: As Manhattan's skyline stretches into the horizon, it mirrors your own potential. You whisper to yourself, "I am limitless," knowing that in the city that never sleeps, there are no boundaries—only endless possibilities.

As we navigate "Inner Dialogue in the City That Never Sleeps," it's impossible not to be reminded of the city's most iconic landmarks—The Statue of Liberty, a symbol of freedom and self-expression; The Guggenheim Museum, a testament to artistic dialogues; and The Apollo Theater, where voices rise and dreams take flight. These landmarks stand as witnesses to the power of conversations with self and Manhattan, where every word spoken within your heart resonates in the city's vibrant tapestry. So, my darlings, let your inner dialogue be your guiding star, a source of inspiration and clarity as you navigate the labyrinth of ambitions. Welcome to The Manhattan Diaries, where every whispered thought becomes a part of your conversation with the city's enduring spirit, an ode to the voice that never stops speaking in the metropolis that never stops dreaming.

Completed Tasks: Inner Dialogue Activities

_____
_____
_____
_____
_____
_____
_____
_____
_____
_____
_____
_____
_____
_____
_____
_____
_____
_____
_____
_____
_____
_____
_____
_____
_____
_____
_____

Inspirational Quote

STEP BY STEP AND THE THING IS DONE. — Charles Atlas

Action Items: Intentions and Thoughts

From Self-Reflection to Rooftop Revelations: The Power of Manhattan Mantras

In the city that reaches for the heavens, where towering skyscrapers kiss the sky, self-reflection becomes an art form—an intimate journey amidst the concrete jungle. Picture it: you, on a rooftop bar overlooking Central Park, surrounded by the city's glittering skyline, experiencing revelations that redefine your path. Join me as we ascend to the heights of "From Self-Reflection to Rooftop Revelations," where Manhattan mantras unlock the power of introspection, becoming the catalyst for a journey of transformation.

➢ **"I Am Exactly Where I Need to Be"**: Surrounded by the dazzling cityscape, you remind yourself that every step, every choice, has led you here. Manhattan teaches you that timing is everything, and right now, you're exactly where you're meant to be.

➢ **"The Sky's Not the Limit—It's Just the Beginning"**: Gazing up at the skyscrapers, you realize that limits are an illusion. In Manhattan, the sky is just a starting point, urging you to dream bigger, reach higher, and expand beyond what you once thought possible.

➢ **"I Define My Own Success"**: From this high vantage point, you see the city's diverse paths to success and realize that your journey is yours alone. Manhattan whispers that success isn't a single destination; it's the confidence to forge your own path.

➢ **"I Embrace My Evolution"**: Standing above it all, you feel the city's constant motion and see it as a reflection of your own journey. In Manhattan, change is celebrated, and every revelation brings you closer to the person you're becoming.

➢ **"I Am Both Soft and Strong"**: Watching the city blend beauty and resilience, you realize your own balance of strength and vulnerability. Manhattan's edges remind you that you can be both delicate and unbreakable—qualities that make you unstoppable.

➢ **"My Journey is as Bold as This View"**: The view from a Manhattan rooftop is bold, daring, and unforgettable—just like your ambitions. Each revelation up here is a reminder that your story deserves to be as fearless as the city itself.

➢ **"I Find Beauty in Every Stage"**: Looking out at the skyline, you appreciate the beauty of every building, each with its own history and evolution. It's a gentle reminder that every phase in your life—like every structure in Manhattan—holds its own magic.

➢ **"I Am My Own North Star"**: With the city lights sparkling around you, you feel a surge of inner clarity. Manhattan's skyline reminds you that while the world is vast, your true direction comes from within—your inner compass guiding you forward.

As we journey through "From Self-Reflection to Rooftop Revelations," it's impossible not to be reminded of the city's most iconic landmarks—The Central Park Reservoir, a tranquil oasis amidst the chaos; The Vessel, a symbol of ascension and self-discovery; and The New York Botanical Garden, where nature and introspection harmonize. These landmarks stand as witnesses to the power of self-reflection and rooftop revelations, where every thought and mantra whispered under the open sky becomes a step toward personal growth. So, my darlings, let your introspection be the guiding star to your rooftop revelations, an affirmation of your commitment to transformation amidst the city's relentless energy. Welcome to The Manhattan Diaries, where every rooftop becomes a stage for your personal journey, and Manhattan mantras lead the way to your own enlightenment, in the city where dreams touch the sky.

Completed Tasks: Self-Reflection Activities

Inspirational Quote

THERE IS NO PASSION TO BE FOUND PLAYING SMALL—IN SETTLING FOR A LIFE THAT IS LESS THAN THE ONE YOU ARE CAPABLE OF LIVING. — Nelson Mandela

Action Items: Intentions and Thoughts

Action Items: Intentions and Thoughts

_____

_____

_____

_____

_____

_____

_____

_____

_____

_____

_____

_____

_____

_____

_____

_____

_____

_____

_____

_____

_____

_____

_____

_____

Fifth Avenue Facials: Starting the Day with a Fresh Face and Fabulous Glow

Manhattan, a city that doesn't just see people—it watches them, taking note of the flushed cheeks after a Central Park jog, or the subtle glow that only comes from a secret skin care sanctuary. In this city where every avenue tells a story, it isn't just about the journey from one skyscraper-shadowed street to another; it's about facing the day with a radiant visage that tells its own tale.

Now, picture this: You're gliding down Fifth Avenue, every storefront reflection showing a face that gleams, a complexion that speaks of care and charisma. That, my dear, isn't just the result of good genes, but the signature Fifth Avenue Facial—a declaration of self-love, an ode to the city's relentless pace yet undying glam.

In this invigorating chapter of The Manhattan Diaries, we'll dive deep into the world of facials that have become the unsung heroes behind those enigmatic Manhattan faces. From steamy deep cleanses that rival the city's summer haze, to the cold laser treatments as thrilling as a December night, you're about to discover the world of opulence that lies behind those spa doors.

But it's not all potions and lotions—no. It's about basking in those fleeting moments of serenity in a city that's constantly on the go. It's about pausing, reflecting, and allowing oneself to be pampered, to emerge refreshed, ready to face the day and its challenges.

Join me, as we embark on this facial journey, from the ritzy salons with views of the park to the hidden gems where whispers of secrets are as common as mask applications. Because, sweetheart, in Manhattan, starting the day right isn't just a mantra, it's a lifestyle. Ready for your close-up? The city's spotlight is on you. Welcome to The Manhattan Diaries—where your face tells a story as captivating as the city's endless saga.

The Art of the Fifth Avenue Glow

In the heart of Manhattan, where every glance could be a paparazzi moment, one thing is essential—the art of the Fifth Avenue Glow. It's not just about walking the streets; it's about facing the world with a radiant, captivating complexion. Picture it: as you stroll down Fifth Avenue, your reflection gleams back at you, speaking of care, charisma, and undeniable glam. This glow isn't just good genes; it's the iconic Fifth Avenue Facial—a ritual of self-love and a tribute to the city's relentless energy. Join me as we uncover the secrets behind this signature glow, the ultimate in Manhattan skincare.

> ➤ **The Power of the Signature Fifth Avenue Facial**: This isn't your typical spa treatment. The Fifth Avenue Facial is a bespoke ritual of exfoliation, hydration, and the perfect touch of glow-boosting magic. It's a must-have for anyone who wants to face the city with radiance that rivals the finest jewels.

> ➤ **Serums That Do More Than Shine**: Manhattanites know that a good serum is worth its weight in gold. Think high-powered, nutrient-packed formulas that brighten, tighten, and give that just-got-back-from-the-Hamptons glow, even if you've been working around the clock.

> ➤ **Luxurious Layers of Hydration**: The secret to that dewy, plump skin? Layers upon layers of hydration. From rich creams to light mists, the Fifth Avenue glow is all about keeping the skin refreshed and radiant, no matter what the city throws your way.

> ➤ **Confidence as the Ultimate Accessory**: The Fifth Avenue Glow isn't just about skincare; it's about the aura. Confidence and self-love radiate from within, giving the skin an extra touch of magic. After all, darling, true glow comes from knowing you're the star of your own Manhattan story.

➢ **The Art of Subtle Highlighting**: It's not just the skin; it's how you enhance it. Manhattan's elite master the art of subtle highlighting, a touch of shimmer here and there that catches the light just so—like the gleam off a diamond bracelet.

➢ **Golden-Hour Glow on Demand**: Fifth Avenue insiders know that a face mist with a hint of illuminating essence can create a golden-hour effect at any time of day. It's like having your own personal lighting crew in a bottle—essential for those all-important coffee dates and boardroom meetings.

➢ **Eye Care for the City's Stamina**: The city never sleeps, but your under-eyes don't have to show it. Manhattan's glow-getters swear by luxurious eye creams and masks to keep the delicate skin around their eyes bright and youthful, even after late nights out.

➢ **Weekly Mask Rituals**: A weekly ritual of detoxifying, hydrating, and illuminating masks is key to maintaining that Fifth Avenue glow. Each mask is like a mini retreat, a moment of self-care amidst the hustle—a way of keeping up appearances while unwinding.

➢ **Signature Scent for the Final Touch**: No Fifth Avenue Glow is complete without a luxurious, lingering fragrance. A hint of a classic, timeless scent wraps you in an invisible aura, leaving a trail of sophistication wherever you go. Because, darling, the glow isn't just what they see—it's what they remember.

In the dazzling world of Manhattan, where every landmark plays a role in our daily drama, the art of the Fifth Avenue Glow is a narrative of empowerment, beauty, and self-expression. As we explore these facets, remember that our radiant faces are the canvas upon which we paint our stories, and the city's endless saga continues to unfold with us at the center stage. Welcome, darlings, to The Manhattan Diaries, where your glow is your passport to the glamorous, ever-evolving tale of this iconic city.

RISE AND SHINE, MANHATTAN STYLE

Completed Tasks: Fifth Avenue Glow Activities

Inspirational Quote

THE WAY TO GET STARTED IS TO QUIT TALKING AND BEGIN DOING. —
Walt Disney

Action Items: Intentions and Thoughts

Opulent Facials: The Hidden Luxury Retreats

In the heart of Manhattan's dazzling landscape, where luxury and glamour reign supreme, there exist hidden sanctuaries of opulence—the coveted facials that are the unsung heroes behind those enigmatic Manhattan faces. In a city that never sleeps, these retreats offer more than just skincare; they provide an escape, a moment of indulgence, and a dose of tranquility amidst the urban chaos. Picture this, darlings: from steamy deep cleanses that rival the city's summer haze to thrilling cold laser treatments as exhilarating as a December night, we are about to embark on a journey through the world of skincare opulence, unveiling the secrets hidden behind those elegant spa doors.

- ➤ **The Signature Deep Cleanse**: This isn't your typical facial—it's a steamy, detoxifying ritual that purifies and revitalizes, leaving skin as fresh as an early morning in Central Park. Perfect for melting away the city's stress and revealing a natural glow.

- ➤ **Diamond-Infused Facials for Pure Radiance**: Nothing says luxury like diamond-infused treatments. These facials polish and illuminate, making you feel as luminous as the Manhattan skyline itself, turning everyday glow into red-carpet radiance.

- ➤ **24-Karat Gold Masks**: A gilded touch for those who demand the best, these 24-karat gold masks infuse the skin with anti-aging magic, lifting and firming with a richness that feels like a tribute to Fifth Avenue's elegance.

- ➤ **The Chilling Cold Laser Therapy**: For the thrill-seekers, cold laser treatments offer a surge of rejuvenation that's as invigorating as a winter walk through the city. It's the ultimate way to tighten, brighten, and keep fine lines at bay.

➢ **Oxygen-Infused Facials for Urban Recovery**: After braving the city's elements, this facial is like a breath of fresh air for your skin. Oxygen-rich serums nourish and plump, reversing the signs of stress and pollution and leaving you radiant.

➢ **Rose Quartz Rollers and Crystal Healing**: These facials incorporate rose quartz and crystal rollers, massaging away tension with the soothing energy of gemstones. It's relaxation meets metaphysical beauty, perfect for aligning your aura and your complexion.

➢ **The "Secret" Lift and Firm Facial**: An exclusive favorite among Manhattan's elite, this lift-and-firm facial combines advanced techniques with indulgent serums, sculpting and contouring the face for a youthful, red-carpet-ready look.

➢ **The 90-Minute Indulgence Escape**: A facial that's as much about relaxation as it is about results. With soothing music, aromatherapy, and gentle hands, this luxurious 90-minute treatment is pure bliss—a hidden retreat from Manhattan's relentless pace.

➢ **Caviar-Infused Hydration**: For the ultimate touch of extravagance, caviar facials deliver intense hydration and nourishment, leaving skin plump, dewy, and utterly radiant. This lavish treatment is like a gourmet feast for the face, adding that unmistakable touch of Manhattan luxury to your glow.

In Manhattan, where every corner holds a story and every landmark becomes a part of our daily drama, the opulent facials hidden within these spa retreats are a testament to our pursuit of beauty and indulgence. As we journey through these facets, remember that skincare is not just a routine; it's an expression of self-love, and the city's relentless pace is balanced by the tranquility found in these luxurious retreats.

Completed Tasks: Hidden Retreats Activities

_____
_____
_____
_____
_____
_____
_____
_____
_____
_____
_____
_____
_____
_____
_____
_____
_____
_____
_____
_____
_____
_____
_____
_____
_____
_____

Inspirational Quote

NEVER COMPLAIN AND NEVER EXPLAIN. — Benjamin Disraeli

Action Items: Intentions and Thoughts

Serenity in the City: The Pampering Pause

In the heart of Manhattan's hustle, there exists a hidden oasis—a place where pampering is more than indulgence; it's a necessity. Imagine this, darlings: a serene spa where time pauses, worries fade, and calm reigns. Join me as we explore these tranquil escapes in the city that never sleeps, where serenity becomes an essential luxury amidst the urban rush.

➢ **The Power of a Calming Ritual**: In Manhattan, a pampering pause is as essential as morning coffee. These rituals—whether a soothing massage or a restorative facial—are crafted to melt away stress and ground you in luxurious calm.

➢ **Customized Aromatherapy Journeys**: Each spa experience begins with a personal touch—a customized blend of essential oils tailored to your mood. It's like a scent passport to relaxation, whisking you to your own private haven.

➢ **Hot Stone Massages for Ultimate Release**: Imagine heated stones gliding across your back, releasing tension with each touch. This indulgent therapy is like a warm hug for the soul, easing out the knots of daily Manhattan life.

➢ **Champagne Soaks for a Glamorous Escape**: A lavish soak in a champagne-infused bath, with bubbles rising around you, is the ultimate way to unwind. It's a splash of opulence that takes relaxation to Manhattan-worthy heights.

➢ **Detoxifying Steam Rooms with a View**: A detoxifying steam session is made even more enchanting with views of the skyline. Surrounded by soft, swirling mist, you release the day's stresses, feeling every pore cleanse and renew as you savor a moment of true urban tranquility.

➢ **Sound Baths for the Urban Soul**: In a city defined by noise, a sound bath is pure luxury. Imagine lying back as healing sound waves wash over you, tuning out the chaos and tuning into a place of deep, blissful calm.

➢ **Hydrating Wraps for Radiant Skin**: City life can be drying, darling, so hydrating body wraps are essential. Wrapped in soft linens infused with moisturizing elixirs, you'll emerge feeling as radiant as the skyline at dusk.

➢ **Facials That Feel Like Rebirth**: These aren't just skincare treatments; they're rejuvenating experiences. Manhattan's elite swear by facials that lift, firm, and restore, turning a pampering pause into a full refresh.

➢ **Mindfulness Moments with Manhattan Views**: Imagine ending your spa day with a cup of herbal tea, gazing at the skyline through floor-to-ceiling windows. It's a quiet moment of reflection, a pause to reconnect before stepping back into the city's pulse.

➢ **Revitalizing Scalp Massages for Instant Clarity**: In a city where ideas never stop, a revitalizing scalp massage is the ultimate brain boost. Each gentle touch clears your mind, leaving you feeling sharp, refreshed, and ready to conquer whatever NYC throws your way.

In the glamorous world of Manhattan, where every landmark plays a part in our daily drama, the pursuit of serenity becomes a testament to our sophistication and our desire for a harmonious balance between ambition and inner peace. As we dive deeper into this world of pampering, remember that serenity isn't just a luxury; it's a precious necessity in the vibrant tapestry of our lives. Welcome to The Manhattan Diaries, my darlings, where serenity becomes a cherished chapter in our glamorous city tale.

Completed Tasks: Pampering Pause Activities

_____
_____
_____
_____
_____
_____
_____
_____
_____
_____
_____
_____
_____
_____
_____
_____
_____
_____
_____
_____
_____
_____
_____

Inspirational Quote

WITHOUT HARD WORK, NOTHING GROWS BUT WEEDS. — Gordon B. Hinckley

Action Items: Intentions and Thoughts

The Manhattan Lifestyle: Starting the Day Right

Ah, the Manhattan lifestyle, where every day is a thrilling act in the never-ending drama of city life. Starting the day right in this bustling metropolis isn't just a routine; it's an art form, a declaration of intent that sets the stage for a day filled with ambition and allure. Picture this, my darlings: the sun rises over Central Park, casting a golden glow upon the city's skyscrapers, and Manhattanites embrace the promise of a new day with grace, style, and audacity. Join me as we dive into the rituals that define the Manhattan lifestyle, from sunrise facials with park views to hidden gems where secrets are exchanged like skincare tips. It's a journey through the glamorous, ever-evolving narrative of the city that never sleeps.

> ➤ **The Sunrise Glow-Up**: Starting the day with a facial that overlooks Central Park isn't just a luxury; it's a commitment to looking as radiant as the sunrise itself. Manhattanites know that great skin is the ultimate power move.

> ➤ **The Art of the Perfect Latte**: In Manhattan, coffee is more than a caffeine fix; it's a statement. Each morning begins with a perfectly crafted latte from a hidden café, setting the tone for a day that's as refined as it is energized.

> ➤ **A Sunrise Stroll in Central Park**: Nothing says "I'm ready to conquer" like a brisk walk through Central Park at dawn. It's a time to breathe, reflect, and prepare for whatever the day may bring—all while surrounded by nature's finest.

> ➤ **A Signature Scent to Begin the Day**: The finishing touch before stepping out—one spritz of a signature perfume that leaves a subtle, unforgettable trail. In Manhattan, your fragrance is as much a part of your presence as your wardrobe, a hint of sophistication that lingers long after you've moved on.

➢ **Dressing for the Day's Stage**: Manhattan mornings are a daily debut, and every outfit is meticulously chosen. From tailored blazers to effortless silk scarves, each piece speaks of purpose, elegance, and a hint of intrigue.

➢ **Exchanging Secrets Over Green Juice**: Wellness meets wit as friends catch up over freshly pressed green juice, sharing stories and trading tips like they're the city's best-kept secrets. It's a blend of gossip and greens that fuels both body and spirit.

➢ **Power Moves and Pilates**: The city's finest start their mornings with a power-packed Pilates class. Strength, flexibility, and focus—the workout mirrors the mindset of every Manhattanite, ready to tackle the day's twists and turns.

➢ **The Iconic Cab Ride Reflection**: A quiet moment in the backseat, gazing at the skyline as the cab winds through the city streets. It's a personal meditation, a chance to set intentions and remind yourself that, yes, you belong here.

➢ **Morning Jazz Soundtrack**: No Manhattan morning is complete without a touch of music. Soft jazz, playing as you get ready, brings a timeless elegance to the routine—a subtle reminder that every day here is its own glamorous story.

In the glamorous world of Manhattan, where every corner holds a story and every landmark plays a part in our daily drama, starting the day right isn't just a mantra; it's a lifestyle, a testament to our ambition and our desire to conquer the world with style and grace. As we navigate these facets of the Manhattan lifestyle, remember that every sunrise in this city is an opportunity to shine, and the spotlight is always on us. Welcome to The Manhattan Diaries, my darlings, where our glamorous narrative unfolds with every sunrise over the iconic landmarks that make this city a true masterpiece of modern life.

Completed Tasks: Day Kickstart Activities

Inspirational Quote

I'D RATHER ATTEMPT TO DO SOMETHING GREAT AND FAIL THAN TO ATTEMPT TO DO NOTHING AND SUCCEED. — Robert H. Schuller

Action Items: Intentions and Thoughts

Action Items: Intentions and Thoughts

Central Park Serenades: Early Morning Walks with the City's Heartbeat

Manhattan, a city that doesn't just witness sunrise—it bathes in its first light, allowing the hues of dawn to paint tales of ambition, dreams, and the intoxicating romance of a new day. And in this urban jungle, there's an oasis where the city doesn't just hustle; it harmonizes—with nature, with whispers of yesteryears, with itself. Ah, Central Park, where every trail isn't about the distance but the moments, memories, and melodies it serenades you with.

Imagine this: You're stepping off Fifth Avenue, the chaos of the city fading as you enter a realm of serene reflections, where the chirping birds and rustling leaves form nature's orchestra. It's not the designer shoes that catch the attention, but the rhythm of your heartbeat syncing with the city's own. That, darling, is the Central Park Serenade—a dance of shadow and light, where every step, every sign, tells a story.

In this lyrical chapter of The Manhattan Diaries, we'll delve into those sun-dappled pathways and misty meadows that make Central Park the heart of Manhattan. From the first dewy footprint on the Bow Bridge to the spirited jog around the Reservoir, we uncover the art of walking with the city's pulse, feeling its every high and low.

But remember, this isn't about mere movement—it's poetry in motion. It's about letting the park's ancient trees whisper secrets, its waters reflect your dreams, its trails map out your ambitions. Embracing both the grandeur of the city's skyline and the intimate whispers of wind-kissed leaves, it's about mastering the dance between Manhattan's modern allure and timeless charm.

So, join me, as we waltz through hidden glades, skip along storied statues, and let the city serenade us with its endless ballad. Because in Manhattan, every dawn is an encore, every path a story waiting to be told. Lace up, love, for the city isn't just awake—it's alive, humming, and waiting for your song.

Welcome to The Manhattan Diaries—where your journey can be as enchanting as the city's ever-evolving melody.

Central Park's Hidden Treasures: Unveiling the Park's Best-Kept Secrets

In the heart of Manhattan, amidst the sprawling urban jungle, lies a sanctuary of serenity and secrets—the iconic Central Park. But oh, my darlings, this is no ordinary park; it's a treasure trove of hidden gems, a tapestry of enchantment waiting to be unveiled. Picture this: meandering pathways leading to picturesque nooks, enchanting bridges whispering tales of yesteryears, and captivating stories that breathe life into every corner. Join me as we embark on a journey to uncover Central Park's best-kept secrets, the charming details that make this urban oasis a romantic hideaway in the midst of the city's hustle and bustle.

- ➤ **The Whispering Bench at Shakespeare Garden**: Nestled in the whimsical Shakespeare Garden, this stone bench is known for its acoustics. Sit at one end, and a friend can hear your softest whispers from the other—it's the perfect spot for sharing secrets under the canopy of trees.

- ➤ **The Hidden Waterfall at The Ramble**: Tucked away in the wild beauty of The Ramble, this little waterfall feels like a slice of nature untouched by the city. With the sound of trickling water and birdsong, it's a secluded retreat that Manhattan's insiders adore.

- ➤ **The Enchanted Bow Bridge**: Iconic, yes, but few know the lore behind Bow Bridge, where countless lovers have whispered promises and shared stolen glances. Its elegant curve makes it the most romantic spot in the park, especially at sunset.

- ➤ **The Secret Garden at Conservatory Garden**: Known for its European-style charm, the Conservatory Garden is a hidden

110

paradise with vibrant blooms, ivy-covered arches, and a quiet elegance. It's where you'll find Manhattan's romantics strolling hand in hand, savoring a moment of calm.

➢ **The Mysterious Glade Arch**: This quaint, stone archway tucked beneath the pathways seems plucked from a fairy tale. It's a perfect spot for a quiet escape, where you can linger in the soft shade and feel as if you've discovered another era entirely.

➢ **The Alice in Wonderland Statue**: A whimsical statue often surrounded by families, but visit early in the morning or late in the evening, and it's all yours. Channel your inner Alice and lose yourself in the fantasy, feeling like a child again amid the city's grown-up glitz.

➢ **The Obscure Balcony at Belvedere Castle**: Perched high above the park, Belvedere Castle offers a balcony view that's often overlooked. It's a breathtaking vantage point where you can gaze over the park's lush greenery and get lost in a view that feels as timeless as Manhattan itself.

➢ **The Bethesda Terrace Mosaics**: Often bustling with people, but those in the know take time to admire the mosaics under Bethesda Terrace. Each tile tells a story, and standing there feels like you're at the heart of Manhattan's artistic soul—a quiet moment of beauty amid the city's rush.

In Manhattan, where every corner holds a story and every landmark becomes a part of our daily drama, Central Park's hidden treasures are a testament to the city's allure and its ability to surprise and captivate at every turn. As we uncover these facets of the park, remember that Central Park isn't just a place; it's a living, breathing character in our daily narrative, and every hidden treasure is a note in the city's symphony. Welcome to The Manhattan Diaries, where secrets become stories, and Central Park's enchantment becomes an integral part of our glamorous city tale.

Completed Tasks: Best Kept Secrets Activities

_____

_____

_____

_____

_____

_____

_____

_____

_____

_____

_____

_____

_____

_____

_____

_____

_____

_____

_____

_____

_____

_____

Inspirational Quote

A CREATIVE MAN IS MOTIVATED BY THE DESIRE TO ACHIEVE, NOT BY THE DESIRE TO BEAT OTHERS. — Ayn Rand

Action Items: Intentions and Thoughts

RISE AND SHINE, MANHATTAN STYLE

Morning Magic: The Art of Sunrise in Central Park

In the enchanting world of Manhattan, where every dawn is an invitation to embrace the city's allure, there exists a magical spectacle that captures the essence of urban romance—the sunrise in Central Park. Oh, my darlings, it's not just about watching the sun paint the sky with hues of gold and crimson; it's about savoring the morning magic, feeling the heartbeat of the city as it awakens to a new day. Picture this: the soft glow of dawn casting a spell over Bow Bridge, the tranquil serenity of the Reservoir, and the symphony of nature harmonizing with Manhattan's skyscrapers. Join me as we explore the art of sunrise in Central Park, a ritual that celebrates the city's timeless charm and its enduring connection with nature.

➢ **Bow Bridge's Golden Embrace**: As the sun rises, Bow Bridge is bathed in a soft, golden light that feels like a scene from a classic romance. Standing there, watching the reflection on the water, it's as if you're part of a timeless Manhattan love story.

➢ **A Stroll Along the Reservoir**: The Jacqueline Kennedy Onassis Reservoir at dawn is a masterpiece of reflection, with the skyline shimmering on its still waters. Morning joggers glide by, adding a pulse to the park's awakening heartbeat—an invigorating start to the day.

➢ **The Cherry Blossoms in Early Spring**: For a few magical weeks, the cherry blossoms transform Central Park into a fairy tale. Catching these delicate pink blooms in the early morning light is a rare treat, a quiet, intimate moment with nature before the city fully stirs.

➢ **Bethesda Terrace's Dawn Symphony**: Imagine the first rays of sunlight hitting the grand arches of Bethesda Terrace. The mosaics glisten, the air feels fresher, and if you're lucky, you might hear a lone musician playing a melody that echoes through the arches—a secret concert just for you.

➤ **The Ramble's Hidden Trails**: At sunrise, The Ramble becomes a quiet sanctuary. Birdsong fills the air, the leaves rustle with the morning breeze, and you can wander through its winding paths as if discovering a hidden world within the city.

➤ **The Boathouse Reflections**: With the sun casting its light over the Boathouse, the lake sparkles in the early morning calm. It's a picture-perfect moment to pause, breathe, and watch the city's silhouette mirrored on the water's surface.

➤ **Sheep Meadow's Morning Serenity**: Before the day's picnics and gatherings, Sheep Meadow is a peaceful open space at dawn. The vast expanse of grass glows with morning dew, offering a rare moment of quiet openness in the heart of Manhattan.

➤ **Belvedere Castle's Sunrise View**: Perched atop the park, Belvedere Castle offers an elevated view that's nothing short of magical at sunrise. From here, you can see the park waking up below and feel as if you're part of a secret morning ritual that's as old as the city itself.

In the enchanting world of Central Park, where every path and bridge becomes a part of your morning tale, experiencing the sunrise is like being part of a timeless Broadway show—the city's charm, its allure, and its endless promise unfolding with each new day. As we delve into these facets, remember that Central Park is not just a place; it's a stage where the city's ever-evolving melody is played out, and you are the star performer. Welcome to The Manhattan Diaries, my darlings, where every sunrise is a serenade to the enduring enchantment of this iconic metropolis.

Completed Tasks: Morning Magic Activities

_____
_____
_____
_____
_____
_____
_____
_____
_____
_____
_____
_____
_____
_____
_____
_____
_____
_____
_____
_____
_____
_____
_____
_____
_____

Inspirational Quote

OPTIMISM IS THE FAITH THAT LEADS TO ACHIEVEMENT. NOTHING CAN BE DONE WITHOUT HOPE AND CONFIDENCE. — Helen Keller

Action Items: Intentions and Thoughts

Central Park's Iconic Landmarks: Sculptures, Fountains, and Historic Tales

In the heart of the bustling concrete jungle that is Manhattan, Central Park stands as a serene oasis, an urban sanctuary where the city's frenetic pace slows down and nature's splendor takes center stage. Within this 843-acre masterpiece, a tapestry of sculptures, fountains, and historic tales unfolds, each telling a story of New York's rich and multifaceted past. As we wander through the verdant pathways of Central Park, let's embark on a journey to discover its iconic landmarks, their hidden secrets, and the tales they whisper to those who take the time to listen.

- ➢ **Bethesda Fountain—The Angel of the Waters**: Standing tall at Bethesda Terrace, this breathtaking fountain isn't just a water feature; it's a symbol of hope and healing. Inspired by the biblical story of the angel blessing the pool of Bethesda, it's a place where Manhattanites come to reflect and find a moment of peace.

- ➢ **Alice in Wonderland Statue**: Tucked near Conservatory Water, this whimsical bronze sculpture captures Alice, the Mad Hatter, and the White Rabbit in all their mischievous glory. It's adored by children and adults alike, a playful reminder of imagination and curiosity at the heart of the city.

- ➢ **Cleopatra's Needle**: This ancient Egyptian obelisk, over 3,000 years old, is one of the park's most fascinating landmarks. Transported from Alexandria to New York, it stands as a testament to history's grandeur—an unexpected piece of ancient wonder in the middle of Manhattan.

- ➢ **The Bow Bridge**: One of the most photographed spots in Central Park, this elegant cast-iron bridge is more than just a pretty view. With its romantic curve and picturesque setting, it's a favorite for lovers, photographers, and dreamers alike—a true Manhattan icon.

➢ **Strawberry Fields—Imagine Mosaic**: A tribute to John Lennon, this serene area near the Dakota is a place of peace and remembrance. With its "Imagine" mosaic, visitors come to honor Lennon's legacy, leaving flowers and tributes in a quiet display of love and memory.

➢ **The Shakespeare Statue**: Found near the Mall, this bronze statue of the Bard himself was dedicated in 1872. Central Park's own tribute to literature's greatest, it's where New Yorkers gather each summer to celebrate the arts with Shakespeare in the Park.

➢ **Belvedere Castle**: Built in 1869, this whimsical Gothic-style castle offers sweeping views of the park and the city beyond. It's a charming place to feel like royalty for a moment, surrounded by breathtaking vistas that are as timeless as the city itself.

➢ **Hans Christian Andersen Statue**: Near Conservatory Water, this statue of the beloved Danish author is a celebration of storytelling. Children gather to hear fairy tales read aloud here, creating a magical connection between generations in the heart of Central Park.

➢ **The Mall and Literary Walk**: This picturesque, elm-lined promenade is home to statues of literary giants, a serene tribute to art and inspiration amidst the bustle of Manhattan.

In the heart of Manhattan, Central Park's iconic landmarks are like pages in a boundless storybook, each one contributing to the rich tapestry of the city's history. These sculptures, fountains, and historic tales speak to the enduring spirit of New York, a place where dreams are realized, heroes are celebrated, and imagination knows no bounds. As we explore these evocative landmarks, we become part of the ever-unfolding narrative of Manhattan, forever intertwined with its vibrant history and timeless charm.

RISE AND SHINE, MANHATTAN STYLE

Completed Tasks: City Park Landmark Activities

Inspirational Quote

NO MATTER HOW MANY GOALS YOU HAVE ACHIEVED, YOU MUST SET YOUR SIGHTS ON A HIGHER ONE. — Jessica Savitch

Action Items: Intentions and Thoughts

The Central Park Lifestyle: Balancing Modernity and Timeless Charm

In the heart of the bustling concrete jungle that is Manhattan, Central Park stands as a serene oasis, an urban sanctuary where the city's frenetic pace slows down and nature's splendor takes center stage. Within this 843-acre masterpiece, a tapestry of sculptures, fountains, and historic tales unfolds, each telling a story of New York's rich and multifaceted past. As we wander through the verdant pathways of Central Park, let's embark on a journey to discover its iconic landmarks, their hidden secrets, and the tales they whisper to those who take the time to listen.

> ➤ **A Morning Run on the Reservoir Loop**: Start the day with a jog around the Jacqueline Kennedy Onassis Reservoir, where the skyline reflects on calm waters. It's the city's chicest cardio, with views that make fitness feel glamorous.

> ➤ **Picnics on Sheep Meadow**: Pack a basket and find your spot on Sheep Meadow—a green expanse that's as fashionable as it is relaxing. From leisurely lunches to sunset picnics, it's the perfect escape for urbanites craving a moment of nature.

> ➤ **Rowboat Romance at the Lake**: Renting a rowboat from Loeb Boathouse is a must. Glide across the lake, under Bow Bridge, and into a scene that feels straight out of a classic Manhattan love story.

> ➤ **Cycling Through the Park's Secret Paths**: A bike ride through the park's winding paths brings out the city's spirit of adventure. Every turn reveals a new view—whether it's hidden sculptures or a surprise garden—making it a journey of discovery.

> ➤ **Afternoon Tea at Tavern on the Green**: Indulge in tea or brunch at this iconic spot, where crystal chandeliers and cozy gardens meet.

It's Manhattan's version of a fairy-tale setting, perfect for sipping and people-watching.

➤ **Sun Salutations at Sunrise**: Early morning yoga on the Great Lawn invites a sense of calm amidst the city's rush. Surrounded by trees and birdsong, it's a mindful escape that feels almost otherworldly.

➤ **Reading by Conservatory Water**: Bring a book and settle by the water, where miniature sailboats glide across. It's a literary escape with a view, a reminder that in Central Park, the simple pleasures are often the finest.

➤ **Jazz Under the Stars**: End the day with live jazz at Bethesda Terrace or Strawberry Fields. With the city skyline twinkling above, these evening concerts bring a touch of timeless charm, blending Manhattan's sophistication with pure, soulful magic.

➤ **The Serenity of The Ramble**: Wander through The Ramble's winding, wooded trails, where you'll feel worlds away from the city's buzz. This quiet enclave invites peaceful reflection and a rare chance to lose yourself in nature, right in the heart of Manhattan.

➤ **Skating at Wollman Rink in Winter**: When winter arrives, there's nothing quite like gliding across Wollman Rink. With the city skyline as your backdrop, this timeless Manhattan experience combines seasonal charm with urban elegance, creating memories as enduring as the park itself.

Central Park's mosaic of sculptures, fountains, and historic tales weaves a narrative that celebrates the resilience, creativity, and human spirit that define Manhattan. Each landmark is a testament to the city's enduring allure and its ability to inspire all who enter its green embrace. As you explore these enchanting sites, you'll find yourself captivated by the stories they hold and the magic they bring to Central Park's enchanting landscape.

Completed Tasks: Modern Timeless Charm Activities

_____

_____

_____

_____

_____

_____

_____

_____

_____

_____

_____

_____

_____

_____

_____

_____

_____

_____

_____

_____

_____

_____

_____

_____

_____

_____

_____

_____

_____

Inspirational Quote

LIFE IS A WORK IN PROGRESS. — Jeff Rich

Action Items: Intentions and Thoughts

Action Items: Intentions and Thoughts

_____

_____

_____

_____

_____

_____

_____

_____

_____

_____

_____

_____

_____

_____

_____

_____

_____

_____

_____

_____

_____

_____

_____

_____

_____

The Breakfast Club: Gourmet Beginnings in the City that Never Sleeps

Manhattan, a city that doesn't just wake up—it rises, glamorous and invigorated, from its fleeting slumber, ready to embrace the heady aroma of roasted coffee, the delicate touch of French pastries, and the vibrant tales of those fortunate enough to call it home. In this city of dreamers, doers, and dawn-breakers, breakfast isn't just the first meal—it's an event, a declaration, an indulgent beginning.

Picture this: You're sauntering down Fifth Avenue, the sun casting a golden glow that rivals the flashiest of boutiques. And while a passerby might be enamored by the boutiques, it's the tantalizing scent wafting from a nearby café that captures you. It's not just about having breakfast, love, it's about owning the moment, starting your day on a high—call it the Manhattan Morning Majesty.

In this delicious chapter of The Manhattan Diaries, we delve into the delectable world of gourmet breakfast that define the city. From the perfect fluffy pancake stacks kissed by Vermont maple syrup, to the artisanal avocado toasts that spell sophistication, to those secret coffee spots where every sip is a rhapsody, we'll embark on a culinary journey like no other.

Yet, it's not just about savoring flavors—it's a symphony of experiences. It's about the charm of watching the city wake up from that corner bistro, or plotting the day's grand plans over a steaming latte. Embracing the skyscrapers' silhouette against the dawn, the hushed conversations of early risers—it's savoring Manhattan's heart and soul, one bite, one sip at a time.

So, take my hand as we hop from hidden gems to opulent diners, as we taste the stories, aspirations, and the sheer brilliance that the city plates up every morning. Because, darling, in Manhattan, every sunrise is an opportunity, and every breakfast, a grand affair. Don your shades, pull up that chair, for the city isn't just serving breakfast—it's dishing out dreams.

Welcome to The Manhattan Diaries—where your mornings set the tone for legendary tales.

The Artistry of Avocado Toast: A Toast to Sophistication

In the bustling heart of Manhattan, where the pulse of the city reverberates through its streets, there's a breakfast sensation that's taken the city's culinary scene by storm: avocado toast. Beyond being a mere meal, it's an art form, a symbol of sophistication that's captured the hearts and palates of Manhattan's discerning breakfast connoisseurs. Join me as we delve into the exquisite world of avocado toast, exploring its rise to prominence and the culinary creativity that defines it.

> ➤ **The Birth of a Breakfast Icon**: Avocado toast didn't just appear; it evolved, transformed from a humble breakfast option into a Manhattan essential. Now, it graces the menu of practically every high-end eatery, its creamy, green slices perfectly perched on artisan bread reflecting the city's knack for transforming the simple into the spectacular.

> ➤ **Avocado Economics**: Delve into the economics behind this 'green gold', and understand why owning that expensive plate of avocado toast is akin to wearing a designer bag to a brunch. In Manhattan's high society, this dish has become less about sustenance and more about status.

> ➤ **Ingredient Alchemy**: Discover the culinary creativity that enhances simple avocado toast into a gourmet experience. From the sprinkle of exotic spices to the drizzle of luxurious truffle oil, chefs across the city are adding their signature twists that turn each bite into a masterpiece.

> ➤ **Celebrity Sightings**: Who's brunching with whom and where can you catch a glimpse? Avocado toast has become a favorite amongst

Manhattan's glitterati, spotted at the trendiest spots, making it the breakfast of choice for those setting the social pace.

➢ **Instagrammable Eats**: Explore how avocado toast won the hearts of Instagram influencers and food bloggers, one aesthetically pleasing snapshot at a time. Each picture-perfect composition showcases not just a meal but a lifestyle, solidifying its place as a social media sensation.

➢ **Chef's Kiss**: Step into the kitchens where culinary geniuses transform everyday ingredients into extraordinary experiences. These chefs are the unsung heroes who meticulously top each slice of toast with perfectly ripe avocados and a hint of culinary genius, making each dish a testament to their artistry.

➢ **Cultural Canvas**: Avocado toast transcends its role as mere food; it's a cultural phenomenon that encapsulates the essence of modern Manhattan living. It's become a symbol of the city's dynamic blend of simplicity and luxury, mirroring the lifestyle of its inhabitants.

➢ **A Taste of Tomorrow**: What lies ahead for the reigning champion of breakfast trends? Peek into the future where culinary innovation continues, predicting what new creations might next captivate the palates of Manhattan's trendy diners. Could anything possibly dethrone the beloved avocado toast? Stay tuned.

As we delight in the artistry of avocado toast, we see the reflection of Manhattan itself—a city that transforms the ordinary into the extraordinary. This simple dish, much like the city's iconic skyline, embodies sophistication and creativity, symbolizing Manhattan's blend of innovation and tradition. Avocado toast isn't just food; it's a celebration of the city's dynamic spirit. So, here's to Manhattan, where each meal is a masterpiece and every bite tells a story of its vibrant essence.

Completed Tasks: Avocado Toast Activities

_____
_____
_____
_____
_____
_____
_____
_____
_____
_____
_____
_____
_____
_____
_____
_____
_____
_____
_____
_____
_____
_____
_____
_____
_____

Inspirational Quote

ALWAYS DO YOUR BEST. WHAT YOU PLANT NOW, YOU WILL HARVEST LATER. — Og Mandino

Action Items: Intentions and Thoughts

The Pancake Chronicles: Fluffy Stacks and Maple Dreams

In the heart of Manhattan, where the city's relentless rhythm is set by the ebb and flow of ambition, there's a culinary phenomenon that embodies the spirit of indulgence and delight: fluffy pancake stacks kissed by Vermont maple syrup. In a city where dreams are as towering as its skyscrapers, these golden wonders have risen to iconic status. Join me as we dive headfirst into the delicious world of pancakes—the Pillars of Pancakedom, if you will—and uncover the secrets behind their irresistible allure.

➤ **Pancake Pinnacle**: Discover how Manhattan's breakfast scene was revolutionized by the humble pancake, transformed into a dish that challenges the ordinary. These stacks rise not just in height but in status, becoming the breakfast of choice for the city's ambitious souls.

➤ **Syrup and Sensibility**: It's not just about the pancakes but the lush drizzle of Vermont maple syrup that crowns them. This syrup isn't merely a topping; it's a declaration of indulgence, turning each bite into a decadent escape from the fast-paced city life.

➤ **Golden Glory**: Each pancake stack is crafted to perfection, resembling the iconic skyscrapers of Manhattan—tall, imposing, and awe-inspiring. These golden-brown delights represent more than a meal; they symbolize the city's endless drive towards culinary excellence.

➤ **Breakfast of Big Dreams**: Amidst the city's ceaseless hustle, pancakes offer a sweet reprieve, a comforting reminder of simpler pleasures. They're not just sustenance but a source of inspiration, fueling the dreams of Manhattanites with each syrupy bite.

➤ **Art on a Plate**: Why settle for ordinary when you can eat art? The aesthetic perfection of these pancakes makes them a favorite subject for food bloggers and Instagram influencers alike, capturing their golden hues and soft, fluffy textures in stunning visual displays.

➢ **Chef's Secrets Revealed**: Step behind the kitchen doors as we reveal the masterful techniques and hidden ingredients that elevate these pancakes to the zenith of brunch cuisine. From the perfect flip to the secret in the batter, learn what makes these pancakes a culinary masterpiece.

➢ **A Bite of Nostalgia**: For many, pancakes evoke deep-seated memories of home and comfort. In Manhattan, these feelings are wrapped in each fluffy layer, providing a nostalgic escape for city dwellers far from their hometowns but close to this newfound comfort food.

➢ **Looking Ahead in Pancakedom**: As Manhattan's culinary scene continues to evolve, what innovations await the beloved pancake? We explore potential future trends that could further elevate this classic dish, from exotic flavor infusions to avant-garde presentation styles, ensuring that pancakes remain a staple in the ever-changing gastronomic landscape of Manhattan.

As we savor the fluffy stacks and maple dreams in the heart of Manhattan, we're reminded that breakfast here is more than just a meal; it's an experience, a celebration of life's possibilities. Pancakes, like the iconic landmarks that define this city, are a testament to the boundless spirit of Manhattan—a place where dreams take shape amidst the towering skyscrapers, and where every bite is a taste of the city's enduring charm. So, let's raise our forks to Manhattan—a city where every morning is a canvas of opportunity, and every pancake is a delicious reminder that greatness is achieved one bite at a time.

Completed Tasks: Pancake Chronicles Activities

_____

_____

_____

_____

_____

_____

_____

_____

_____

_____

_____

_____

_____

_____

_____

_____

_____

_____

_____

_____

_____

_____

Inspirational Quote

OUR GREATEST WEAKNESS LIES IN GIVING UP. THE MOST CERTAIN WAY TO SUCCEED IS ALWAYS TO TRY JUST ONE MORE TIME. — Thomas A. Edison

Action Items: Intentions and Thoughts

Hidden Gems: Manhattan's Best-Kept Breakfast Secrets

In the glittering heart of Manhattan, where the city's surface dazzles with well-known icons, there exists a secret world—an underworld of hidden breakfast gems known only to a chosen few. These are the elusive places, the tucked-away corners, where locals and the savviest visitors discover a Manhattan less traveled, where breakfast is an art form, a secret handshake, a whispered promise. Join me as we embark on a clandestine journey through the city's best-kept breakfast secrets, where the magic of Manhattan lies not in the spotlight, but in the shadows.

- ➤ **Whispered Culinary Confidences**: Venture into the secretive realm of Manhattan's breakfast scene, where elite diners and in-the-know locals share hushed conversations about hidden spots. These cherished places offer more than just food; they are gateways to a clandestine world where every meal feels like an exclusive invitation.

- ➤ **The Secret Menu Mystique**: Dive into the intriguing world of secret menus and undisclosed dishes that transform an ordinary breakfast into an exhilarating culinary adventure. In these select eateries, the thrill lies in discovering flavors that aren't listed, offering a unique experience that feels both personal and privileged.

- ➤ **Hidden Havens**: Discover the magic of tucked-away eateries hidden in plain sight among Manhattan's bustling streets. These are the spots where true breakfast aficionados find solace, indulging in the art of the first meal of the day in settings that feel like well-kept secrets.

- ➤ **Locals Only**: Gain entry to the inner circle of true New Yorkers who skip the well-trodden tourist paths to savor breakfasts that are as authentically Big Apple as yellow cabs and Broadway lights. These are the places where locals recharge, reflect, and relish the city's dynamic spirit in the quiet morning hours.

➤ **Cafe Incognito**: Explore the charm of hidden cafes where the city's cultural and financial luminaries meet. These spots offer a sanctuary from the public eye, where influential figures enjoy their morning rituals surrounded by an air of tranquility and exclusivity.

➤ **Breakfast at Hidden Tiffany's**: Picture a breakfast so exclusive and hidden, it could be the backdrop for a Truman Capote novel. Here, luxury meets secrecy in intimate settings where every table has a story, and every dish is served with a side of glamour and mystery.

➤ **Underground Flavors**: Take a journey below the surface of Manhattan's polished exterior to discover the underground breakfast trends that are setting the pace for the culinary avant-garde. These flavors redefine morning dining, offering bold and unexpected twists that challenge conventional breakfast norms.

➤ **A Toast to the Unseen**: Celebrate Manhattan's lesser-known culinary gems with a toast (or a cup of finely brewed coffee) to the hidden breakfast spots that offer more than just food—they provide a passage to the heart of the city's vibrant culture and the unspoken promise of Manhattan's endless possibilities.

As we uncover Manhattan's best-kept breakfast secrets, we realize that the city's magic isn't just in its towering landmarks but also in the hidden corners where culinary treasures await. These clandestine spots are like the hidden speakeasies of the Jazz Age, where breakfast is a whispered promise, a secret society of flavors. Just as the city's secrets are held in the whispers of its history, these breakfast gems are whispers of flavor, inviting us to savor Manhattan's mystery, one bite at a time. So, let's raise our cups of coffee to this clandestine world within the city, where every meal is a discovery, and every bite is a well-guarded secret. Welcome to The Manhattan Whispers, where the hidden gems shine as brightly as the skyscrapers that grace our skyline.

Completed Tasks: Hidden Gem Activities

_____

_____

_____

_____

_____

_____

_____

_____

_____

_____

_____

_____

_____

_____

_____

_____

_____

_____

_____

_____

_____

_____

_____

_____

_____

_____

_____

Inspirational Quote

EITHER YOU RUN THE DAY, OR THE DAY RUNS YOU. — Jim Rohn

Action Items: Intentions and Thoughts

Java Journeys" The Art of Manhattan's Coffee Culture

In the heart of Manhattan, where the city pulses with energy and ambition, there's a cultural phenomenon that flows through its veins—an obsession that unites Wall Street moguls and struggling artists alike: coffee. It's not just a beverage; it's a way of life, a daily ritual that fuels the dreams and ambitions of New Yorkers. Join me as we embark on a journey through the art of Manhattan's coffee culture—Java Journeys, if you will—where every cup is a sip of inspiration, a conversation starter, and a reminder that in this city, anything is possible with the right brew.

➢ **Brewed Ambition**: Delve into the essence of Manhattan's coffee culture, where the high-octane energy of Wall Street bankers and the vibrant creativity of East Village artists converge in their mutual need for caffeine. Here, coffee isn't just a beverage; it's the fuel for a city's dreams and ambitions, powering a bustling metropolis from dawn until dusk.

➢ **Artistic Espresso**: Step into the eclectic coffee shops scattered throughout Manhattan, where the espresso shots are as finely crafted as the artwork hanging on the walls. These cafes serve as sanctuaries for the city's creative minds, offering a space where writers, painters, and musicians draw inspiration from the rich, bold flavors of expertly brewed coffee.

➢ **Caffeinated Conversations**: Explore how Manhattan's myriad coffee spots foster social interactions that are as stimulating as the coffee itself. From spontaneous business meetings to deep philosophical discussions, coffee tables in this city are platforms for connection, debate, and partnership.

➢ **Beans of the Big Apple**: Trace the journey of Manhattan's beloved coffee beans, from their origins in distant, sun-drenched fields to their transformation into the perfect brew in a bustling local coffee shop. This segment highlights the global connections and meticulous sourcing that contribute to the unique coffee culture of New York.

➢ **Latte Luxuries**: Indulge in the luxurious world of the perfect latte, where skilled baristas transform the simple combination of espresso and milk into a silky, frothy art form. Witness the precision and creativity involved in crafting latte art, making each cup a personal masterpiece that delights both the eyes and the palate.

➢ **Coffee Shop Chronicles**: Visit the landmark coffeehouses of Manhattan that have stood the test of time, becoming as much a part of the city's fabric as its towering skyscrapers and bustling subways. These establishments chart the historical and cultural evolution of coffee, showcasing its rise from a mere morning kick-starter to a revered icon of urban lifestyle.

➢ **Barista Buzz**: Meet the charismatic and skilled baristas who are the heart and soul of Manhattan's coffee scene. Celebrated not just for their coffee-making skills but also for their ability to brighten customers' days, these coffee experts are local celebrities in their own right, each adding a personal touch that turns a simple coffee run into an anticipated daily ritual.

As we delve into Manhattan's coffee culture, we discover it's more than a drink—it's a lifestyle and a beacon of the city's drive for perfection. Coffeehouses serve as daily landmarks where dreams take shape over steaming cups of java, echoing the city's iconic skyline. They remind us that in Manhattan, the possibilities are as limitless as the steam from a fresh cappuccino. So, let's toast with our coffee cups to Manhattan—a city where every sip inspires dreams and every coffeehouse tells a story of vibrant culture. Welcome to Java Journeys, where each coffee break is a journey of discovery and connection in the city that never sleeps.

Completed Tasks: Java Journey Activities

Inspirational Quote

WE MAKE THE WORLD WE LIVE IN AND SHAPE OUR OWN ENVIRONMENT.
— Orison Swett Marden

Action Items: Intentions and Thoughts

Breakfast with a View: Manhattan's Skyline and Sunrise

In the grand theater of Manhattan, where dreams are born and ambitions reach for the stars, there exists a breakfast experience that transcends mere sustenance—it's breakfast with a view. Picture this: the city's skyline, bathed in the golden hues of dawn, while you savor the first bites of your morning meal. Join me as we embark on a journey through the world of breakfast spots that offer not only delicious cuisine but also a front-row seat to Manhattan's iconic skyline and sunrise—a breakfast where the view is as delectable as the food.

> ➤ **Sky-High Flavors**: Begin your morning in the grand theater of Manhattan, where the breakfast scene is elevated literally to new heights. High above the city streets, chic rooftop cafes serve up culinary delights paired with a side of stunning skyline views, transforming your breakfast into a magical experience that awakens all senses.

> ➤ **Dawn's Early Light**: Relish the serene beauty of early morning Manhattan, where the first light bathes iconic skyscrapers in a warm glow. Enjoy a front-row seat to this daily spectacle, savoring gourmet dishes as the city unfolds beneath the rising sun, offering a peaceful contrast to the bustling day ahead.

> ➤ **Epicurean Heights**: Explore the pinnacle of dining experiences at select venues perched atop Manhattan's towering buildings. Here, every meal is both a visual and gastronomic feast, with panoramic views that stretch across the city, enhancing your dining experience with every bite.

> ➤ **Golden Hour Gastronomy**: Experience breakfast during the golden hour when every corner of Manhattan glimmers with the promise of a new day. Dine on meticulously prepared dishes that

seem all the more delicious under the soft, flattering light of dawn that illuminates the city's famous skyline.

➤ **Windows on Manhattan**: Choose from a variety of breakfast spots designed with expansive windows and open terraces that offer a breathtaking backdrop of Manhattan's architectural marvels. These restaurants provide a spectacular setting to enjoy the city as it wakes, a perfect complement to a meticulously curated morning menu.

➤ **Luxury on a Plate**: Indulge in the ultimate luxury breakfast experience where the elegance of the cuisine rivals the splendor of the surrounding cityscape. Each meal is a testament to sophisticated dining, designed to harmonize with the awe-inspiring views of Manhattan's skyline, creating a symphony of exquisite flavors and sights.

➤ **Celebrity Morning Rituals**: Take part in a morning tradition favored by Manhattan's elite. These exclusive breakfast venues are not just about food; they're about being seen in the right places, enjoying sumptuous meals while the city's skyline provides a spectacular backdrop, echoing the heights of their ambitions.

As we enjoy breakfast with a view in Manhattan, we recognize that here, every meal is an event, celebrating the city's commitment to excellence. Iconic as the skyline itself, these breakfast spots offer not only spectacular food but also stunning views, reminding us that even a morning meal can be a moment of reflection and inspiration. In this city of ceaseless ambition, each sunrise and breakfast spot presents an opportunity to appreciate the beauty around us and the limitless potential of new beginnings. Let's toast to Manhattan—a city where every morning brings new possibilities and every breakfast is a front-row seat to its dynamic allure. Welcome to Breakfast with a View, where each meal honors the grandeur of Manhattan, a city that dreams as boldly as it lives.

Completed Tasks: Breakfast with a View Activities

Inspirational Quote

MOTIVATION WILL ALMOST ALWAYS BEAT MERE TALENT. — Norman Ralph Augustine

Action Items: Intentions and Thoughts

_____
_____
_____
_____
_____
_____
_____
_____
_____
_____
_____
_____
_____
_____
_____
_____
_____
_____
_____
_____
_____
_____
_____
_____
_____
_____
_____
_____
_____
_____
_____
_____

Action Items: Intentions and Thoughts

Dawn's Designer Diary:
Crafting a Day's Ensemble with Panache

Manhattan, a city that doesn't merely admire—it critiques, lauds, and occasionally gasps in sheer wonderment. In this grid of ambitions and aspirations, it's not about merely wearing clothes—it's about curating ensembles that tell tales, evoke emotions, and, let's be honest, turn more than a few heads. Because here, fashion isn't just personal—it's a proclamation.

Envision yourself: Stepping onto Fifth Avenue, and while sequins might glitter and silks might shimmer, what truly captivates isn't sewn on a label—it's stitched into the very fabric of your persona. That, darling, is the Manhattan Ensemble Extravaganza, an art form that's less about the clothes and more about the story they narrate. A performance that starts with the swish of a skirt and ends with a standing ovation.

In this fabulously stylish chapter of The Manhattan Diaries, we pull back the velvet curtains on the art of dressing with audacity. From the vintage finds tucked away in hidden boutiques to the audacious modern cuts from ateliers that define the now, you'll discover how to craft a day's look that doesn't just complement you—it defines you.

But it's not just about drapes and cuts. Oh no, it's about harmonizing with the city's rhythm, orchestrating a day's look that dances with Manhattan's pace, matches its beat, and, on occasion, outshines its many lights. It's the allure of blending with the city's shadows and yet standing out in its bright squares, understanding and embodying the city's pulse.

So, accompany me, as we journey through ateliers and back-alley boutiques, where sequins meet stories, and fabrics fuse with fantasies. Because, darling, in Manhattan, every morning is a blank canvas and every ensemble, a masterpiece waiting to be showcased. Grab that clutch, slip into those heels, for the city doesn't just need a look—it craves a performance.

Welcome to The Manhattan Diaries—where your style becomes as legendary as the city's chronicles.

Vintage Treasures: Unearthing Manhattan's Fashion Secrets

In the heart of Manhattan, where the city's skyline glitters with ambition, there exists a hidden world of fashion treasures waiting to be unearthed. The art of dressing here is more than just donning clothes; it's about discovering vintage gems that whisper tales of eras gone by. Picture this: wandering through the hidden boutiques and timeworn shops that line the city's streets, where each piece tells a story, and every garment is a piece of history. Join me as we embark on a journey to uncover Manhattan's fashion secrets— where the past and present collide in a sartorial dance that defines the city's unique style.

➢ **Vintage Chic**: Darling, imagine strolling down Manhattan's streets and discovering chic boutiques that hold the key to a bygone era's fashion secrets. These hidden gems offer carefully curated collections of vintage clothing and accessories that will transport you through time, from the elegant flapper dresses of the roaring twenties to the iconic mid-century suits that defined an era.

➢ **Fashion History Lessons**: Every piece you find in these boutiques has a story to tell, and some shopkeepers are more than happy to share the tales behind their treasures. Picture yourself not just picking out a fabulous garment but also learning about the intriguing narratives that make each piece even more fascinating.

➢ **Mix and Match Magic**: Now, darling, let's talk about the art of mixing vintage treasures with contemporary fashion to create a style that's as unique as you are. It's about blending the old and the new, creating ensembles that capture the essence of Manhattan's ever-evolving spirit while making a statement that's entirely your own.

➢ **Era-Inspired Elegance**: Dive headfirst into the world of era-inspired fashion. Whether you want to channel the roaring twenties' glamour, the 1950s' sophistication, or the boldness of the 1980s, vintage pieces allow you to step back in time while strutting confidently into the present. It's like being a fashion time traveler, sweetie!

➢ **Thrifting Adventures**: Are you ready for a fabulous thrifting adventure, my dear? Manhattan's thrift shops are simply waiting for you to uncover their hidden treasures. Imagine the thrill of discovering unique finds and embracing the excitement of the hunt for that perfect vintage gem.

➢ **Personalized Styling**: Some vintage shops offer personalized styling services that will elevate your fashion game to new heights. They help you curate ensembles that not only reflect your unique personality but also pay homage to Manhattan's rich fashion history. It's like having your very own fashion fairy godmother, guiding you towards impeccable style.

As we delve into Manhattan's vintage fashion scene, we uncover a world where clothing isn't just fabric; it's a portal to another time and a unique form of self-expression. Much like the iconic landmarks that grace this city's skyline, these vintage treasures are landmarks of sartorial splendor. They remind us that in Manhattan, fashion is an ever-evolving art form, a reflection of our individuality, and an homage to the city's enduring allure. So, let's celebrate Manhattan's vintage secrets, where each garment is a chapter in the city's stylish chronicles, and every outfit tells a story of timeless elegance. Welcome to Vintage Treasures, where the past meets the present, and your style becomes an unforgettable part of Manhattan's fashionable history, darling.

Completed Tasks: Vintage Treasures Activities

_____
_____
_____
_____
_____
_____
_____
_____
_____
_____
_____
_____
_____
_____
_____
_____
_____
_____
_____
_____
_____
_____
_____
_____

Inspirational Quote

THE MOST EFFECTIVE WAY TO DO IT, IS TO DO IT. — Amelia Earhart

Action Items: Intentions and Thoughts

Runway to Real Life: Embracing Manhattan's Haute Couture

In Manhattan, where ambition is woven into the very fabric of the city, fashion transcends art—it becomes a bold statement. Step into the world of Manhattan's haute couture, where runway dreams are transformed into everyday realities on vibrant streets. Each outfit embodies the city's dynamic essence. Join us in exploring "Runway to Real Life," where the audacity of modern cuts and avant-garde designs come alive. Learn to infuse high fashion into your daily look in a city where style not only reflects but defines its unstoppable rhythm.

> **Couture on the Sidewalks**: Venture into Manhattan's streets, where haute couture is not confined to exclusive events but worn daily by those striding along avenues and alleys. Here, high fashion blends seamlessly with the urban landscape, transforming every sidewalk into a runway where style meets spontaneity.

> **Fashion as Statement**: In the heart of Manhattan, fashion is more than art—it's a bold declaration of individuality and ambition. Each outfit tells a story of aspiration and achievement, acting as a wearable manifesto of the city's relentless drive and dynamic spirit.

> **From Catwalk to Crosswalk**: Delve into the skillful artistry of Manhattan's fashion-forward residents who adeptly translate haute couture from the glamorous runways to the gritty reality of streetwear. Learn how every crosswalk becomes a stage for personal expression, showcasing the latest trends with a unique city twist.

> **Avant-Garde Everyday**: Explore the methods by which Manhattan's style enthusiasts incorporate audacious modern cuts and pioneering designs into their daily wardrobe. Discover how avant-garde fashion becomes an accessible and integral part of everyday life, pushing the boundaries of typical day-to-day attire.

➢ **The Rhythm of Style**: Understand how Manhattan's fashion beats in sync with the rhythm of the city—fast-paced, fearless, and unapologetically ahead of the curve. Fashion here is as vibrant and fluid as the city itself, embodying the essence of New York's bold character.

➢ **Accessorizing with Grit and Glamour**: Master the art of accessorizing in a city that adores both grit and glamour. In Manhattan, the perfect accessory can make or break an outfit, serving as a powerful statement piece that reflects both the wearer's style and the city's architectural grandeur.

➢ **Iconic Inspirations**: Gain inspiration from the luminaries of Manhattan's fashion scene. From the enduring elegance of historical trendsetters to the innovative designs of contemporary couturiers, these fashion icons continuously shape the city's narrative, offering new visions of what fashion can signify.

➢ **Empowering Ensembles**: Choose ensembles that not only showcase personal style but also empower the wearer. In Manhattan, clothing is an armor and adornment, reflecting personal strength and resilience in a city that epitomizes reinvention and renewal. Here, each outfit is a testament to the wearer's confidence and the city's undying vibrancy.

In "Runway to Real Life," Manhattan's fashion transcends mere clothing—it's a canvas for self-expression and a beacon of the city's spirit. Haute couture mirrors the iconic skyline, shaping both style's present and future. These designs are not just garments but timeless art, reflecting our identities and celebrating Manhattan's relentless ambition. Let's toast to this city's fashion legacy, where every piece is a masterpiece and your style becomes as iconic as Manhattan itself. Welcome to "Runway to Real Life," where couture is part of your everyday narrative.

Completed Tasks: Runway to Real Life Activities

Inspirational Quote

TO BE ABLE TO LOOK BACK UPON ONE'S PAST LIFE WITH SATISFACTION IS TO LIVE TWICE. — John Dalberg-Acton

Action Items: Intentions and Thoughts

RISE AND SHINE, MANHATTAN STYLE

Street Style Chronicles: Fashion that Echoes Manhattan's Pulse

In the vibrant pulse of Manhattan, where creativity and ambition thrive, fashion transcends mere clothing—it becomes a powerful form of self-expression, resonating with the city's rhythm. Imagine walking the bustling streets, where each passerby's outfit turns the sidewalks into runways. Welcome to "Street Style Chronicles," where dressing is an art that mirrors the dynamic spirit of Manhattan. Here, fashion is not just about garments; it's about embodying the city's essence in every ensemble. Join us as we delve into the captivating world of street style, where every outfit tells a story.

- ➤ **Sidewalk as Runway**: Venture into Manhattan's bustling avenues where the sidewalks transform into unofficial runways. Here, each passerby is a model in their own right, showcasing personal style that captures the city's eclectic and vibrant fashion scene. Every step taken is a statement of self, blending seamlessly with the urban backdrop.

- ➤ **Echoes of Ambition**: Observe how the palpable ambition of Manhattan's residents is intricately stitched into their streetwear. Outfits are bold and daring, reflecting the city's ethos of reaching for the stars. Each garment worn on the street mirrors the wearer's personal goals and the collective drive of this metropolis.

- ➤ **Fashion as Dialogue**: Delve deep into the heart of Manhattan where fashion becomes a potent form of communication. Here, each ensemble is a conversation starter, speaking volumes about the wearer's identity, lifestyle, and cultural influences without a single word being exchanged.

- ➤ **The Pulse of Creativity**: Explore how the relentless creativity that throbs through Manhattan influences its street style. Witness how everyday clothing choices evolve into a dynamic exhibition of textures, colors, and silhouettes, each reflecting the vibrant diversity of the city itself.

➤ **Iconic Inspirations**: Uncover the sartorial choices inspired by the city's iconic landmarks and pivotal cultural moments. In Manhattan, fashion intersects with urban life to forge outfits that are as memorable as the city's skyline, parks, and bustling city corners.

➤ **Trends on the Move**: Keep pace with the rapidly evolving fashion trends that ripple through the streets of Manhattan. These trends often set the global tempo for style, pioneering looks that eventually grace magazines and populate social media feeds worldwide.

➤ **Personal Style Diaries**: Meet the local fashion influencers and sartorial innovators who turn their daily outfits into a public diary. Through blogs, Instagram, and other social media platforms, these style mavens document their fashion journey, influencing others and setting trends in real-time.

➤ **A Canvas of Self-Expression**: Embrace street style as the ultimate canvas for personal expression in Manhattan. Here, every sartorial choice is a declaration of independence, creativity, and personal narrative, played out against the backdrop of one of the world's most dynamic cities.

In "Street Style Chronicles," we dive into a world where fashion is the language of New Yorkers, each outfit telling its unique story. Manhattan's streets become vibrant canvases, reflecting the city's dynamic identity. This series shows that style is more than clothing—it's a living art form that mirrors our inner selves and the city's relentless expression. Let's celebrate Manhattan's street style, where every sidewalk is a runway, every passerby a muse. Welcome to "Street Style Chronicles," where your style pulses with the vibrant rhythm of this extraordinary city.

Completed Tasks: Street Style Chronicles Activities

_____
_____
_____
_____
_____
_____
_____
_____
_____
_____
_____
_____
_____
_____
_____
_____
_____
_____
_____
_____
_____
_____
_____
_____

Inspirational Quote

LIFE IS A TIDE; FLOAT ON IT. GO DOWN WITH IT AND GO UP WITH IT BUT BE DETACHED. THEN IT IS NOT DIFFICULT. — Prem Rawat

Action Items: Intentions and Thoughts

Fashion as Performance: The Art of Turning Heads in Manhattan

In the glittering theater that is Manhattan, where every street corner is a stage, fashion isn't just about clothes—it's a performance, a statement, an art form that commands attention. Imagine stepping onto the city's grandest boulevards, where the applause isn't reserved for Broadway alone. It's the art of turning heads, darling, and making every day a showstopper. Welcome to "Fashion as Performance," where the streets of Manhattan become your runway, and dressing up is more than a daily ritual—it's an act of theater that rivals the grandest productions in town.

> ➤ **Center Stage on Fifth Avenue**: Take your fashion cues from Broadway as you strut down Manhattan's grand boulevards. In this city, every step is a moment in the spotlight, every sidewalk a runway, where your style choices garner the kind of applause usually reserved for theater stars.

> ➤ **Dress Rehearsals No More**: Forget the notion of dress rehearsals; in Manhattan, every day is opening night. Dress with the intention to dazzle from dawn till dusk, turning daily outings into premiere events where your ensemble shines as the star of the show.

> ➤ **Couture Costumes**: Elevate your daily wardrobe to the level of theatrical costumes in the grand drama of Manhattan. Each piece of clothing is a brushstroke in a masterful painting, each accessory a carefully chosen prop that adds depth and character to your personal narrative.

> ➤ **Applause-Worthy Accessories**: Choose accessories that do more than complement—they captivate. Like a show-stopping number in a hit musical, your details should draw eyes and command attention, making every gesture a dramatic flourish that enhances your overall performance.

➢ **Dramatic Entrances Guaranteed**: In Manhattan, the art of making an entrance is paramount. Treat each arrival as a grand reveal, ensuring your fashion makes a statement bold enough to match the city's imposing architecture and vibrant scenes.

➢ **Encore Performances**: In the city's fashion theater, a successful outfit demands an encore. Cultivate a wardrobe that keeps the audience—the city's discerning onlookers—eager for your next appearance, with styles that are continually fresh and exhilarating.

➢ **Standing Ovation Style**: Aspire to assemble outfits that not only turn heads but stop traffic, much like a standing ovation at the end of a Broadway hit. Your fashion should leave a mark, memorable enough to linger in the minds of passersby long after you've exited the scene.

➢ **Curtain Call Chic**: Conclude your day with the same flair with which you started it, ensuring your evening ensemble is as striking and unforgettable as the closing scene of a Broadway spectacular. In Manhattan, every night should end with a fashion statement that feels like a poignant curtain call, leaving onlookers in awe and anticipation for your next show.

In "Fashion as Performance," we discover that in Manhattan, every outfit is a costume, every corner a stage, and every day a new scene. Like the city's iconic landmarks, fashion is a dynamic performance that reflects our personalities and pays homage to Manhattan's artistic spirit. It reminds us that here, every moment is a chance to dazzle and every look can capture the spotlight. Let's toast to the grand stage of Manhattan, where every step is an expression of self and every ensemble earns applause. Welcome to "Fashion as Performance," where your style shines bright and becomes an integral part of the city's vibrant story.

Completed Tasks: Performance Fashion Activities

Inspirational Quote

NOTHING IS MORE PRECIOUS THAN LIFE . . . ESPECIALLY THE LIFE OF YOUR CHILD. — Peter Diamandis

Action Items: Intentions and Thoughts

Action Items: Intentions and Thoughts

_____

_____

_____

_____

_____

_____

_____

_____

_____

_____

_____

_____

_____

_____

_____

_____

_____

_____

_____

_____

_____

_____

_____

_____

_____

_____

_____

_____

Yoga with a Cityscape: Stretching to the Skyline's Tune

Manhattan, a city that doesn't simply pulse—it breathes, with the synchronized rhythm of aspirations, heartbeats, and the gentle hum of the morning's meditation. Here, amidst the high-rises and high hopes, it isn't just about charting a journey; it's about grounding oneself while reaching for the skies, blending the serenity of the soul with the drive of the city.

Picture this: You're on a rooftop, not far from Fifth Avenue. The sun paints soft hues across the horizon, the skyline a silhouette against dawn's embrace. As you move into your warrior pose, it isn't the designer logo on your yoga mat that captures attention, but the grace with which you mirror the city's skyline. That, darling, is the Manhattan Stretch—a dance of poise, peace, and infinite potential.

In this introspective chapter of The Manhattan Diaries, we delve deep into the world of urban zen. From the tranquil whispers of sunrise salutations amid skyscraper shadows to the empowering force of a vinyasa with views of the cityscape, you'll learn to channel Manhattan's energy into a flow that is uniquely yours.

But this journey isn't merely about asanas and postures. No. It's about aligning with the city's essence, harmonizing with its ebb and flow, and turning its cacophonous symphony into a soothing lullaby. It's about realizing that between the vastness of the Hudson and the magnificence of the Empire State, there lies a space—a sanctum—where the city's heart and your soul resonate.

So, come with me, as we discover rooftop retreats and balcony sanctuaries, where the city's pulse becomes the very rhythm of our breaths. Because, sweetheart, in Manhattan, every sunrise is an invitation to not just witness, but to become—a part of its grand tapestry. Roll out that mat, for the city is not just the backdrop; it's the muse. Welcome to The Manhattan Diaries—where your flow, much like the city's skyline, knows no bounds.

Sunrise Serenity: Yoga with a Manhattan View: Elevate Your Practice

Imagine this, darlings: Yoga as a poetic dance with Manhattan's skyline. Each sunrise from a Fifth Avenue rooftop invites you to elevate your practice among the towering cityscape. As the sun casts its soft hues over the city, your morning yoga transcends mere routine, becoming a graceful reflection of the urban landscape. This is the essence of "Sunrise Serenity: Yoga with a Manhattan View"—where every movement harmonizes with the city's heartbeat.

➢ **Skyline Salutations**: Begin your day with sun salutations against the breathtaking backdrop of Manhattan's iconic skyline. As you stretch towards the sky, align your body and spirit with the towering silhouettes of the city's most famous structures, each pose becoming a reflection of the urban grandeur around you.

➢ **Elevated Asanas**: Elevate your yoga practice to extraordinary heights on a rooftop overlooking Fifth Avenue. Surrounded by the architectural marvels of Manhattan, each asana feels like a step closer to the heavens, enhancing both your physical and spiritual experience amidst the cityscape.

➢ **Dawn's Early Light**: Embrace the serene beauty of a Manhattan sunrise, where the early light bathes the city in ethereal hues. This magical moment enhances your morning routine, invigorating your soul and providing a stunning visual meditation as the city slowly comes to life.

➢ **Urban Zen**: Discover a unique peace above the hustle and bustle, finding your zen at the heart of the city. As Manhattan wakes up below, you can enjoy a tranquil respite on your mat, blending the urban energy with mindful serenity in each breath and movement.

➢ **Style and Stretch**: Complement your yoga practice with stylish gear that reflects the elegance and sophistication of Manhattan. Whether it's the designer logo on your mat or the sleek cut of your attire, make your morning routine a chic and fashionable statement that captures the essence of city life.

➢ **Architectural Harmony**: Flow through your yoga poses with the poise and grace of the nearby skyscrapers. Your movements and the urban landscape enter into a dance of architectural harmony, creating a visual and physical symmetry that inspires both awe and inner calm.

➢ **Sky-High Serenity**: As you hold each pose, capture the essence of tranquility and ambition from your unique vantage point above the city that never sleeps. Experience a rare calm as you overlook the awakening metropolis, with the morning sky's changing colors providing a perfect canvas for reflection.

➢ **Metropolitan Meditation**: Conclude your yoga session with a deep meditation that channels the dynamic energy of Manhattan. As the city stirs beneath you, let its vibrant pulse set a motivated yet peaceful tone for your day, reminding you of the endless possibilities that await after your mat is rolled away.

In "Sunrise Serenity: Yoga with a Manhattan View," we find tranquility and ambition intertwined, as our breath syncs with the city's vibrant pulse. Amidst iconic skyscrapers, yoga becomes a profound connection to urban life, offering a sanctuary amidst the hustle. Here, every sunrise invites you to join Manhattan's grand narrative. Welcome to "Sunrise Serenity," where your yoga practice elevates to match the city's soaring skyline, merging seamlessly with the soul of Manhattan.

Completed Tasks: Yoga with a View Activities

Inspirational Quote

WE MAY ENCOUNTER MANY DEFEATS, BUT WE MUST NOT BE DEFEATED.
— Maya Angelou

Action Items: Intentions and Thoughts

Sunrise Serenity: Yoga with a Manhattan View: Dawn's Embrace

Darlings, let's dive into a world where the serenity of sunrise meets the dynamic energy of Manhattan—a city that not only pulses but breathes in synchronized harmony with your aspirations. Imagine, if you will, a rooftop session not far from the illustrious Fifth Avenue. The sun, still in its slumber, begins to paint soft hues across the horizon, casting a magical spell on the iconic skyline. As you gracefully flow through your morning yoga routine, it's not the designer logo on your mat that captures attention, but the elegance with which you mirror the city's dawn embrace. This, my loves, is "Dawn's Embrace: Yoga with a Manhattan View."

➢ **Skyline Silhouettes**: Start your morning amidst the awe-inspiring silhouettes of Manhattan's towering skyscrapers. As you settle into each pose, let the iconic skyline shape the backdrop of your practice, enhancing the tranquility and grandeur of your sunrise yoga.

➢ **Elegance in Asanas**: Embrace the elegance of Manhattan's dawn as you flow through your yoga routine. Each movement is a graceful homage to the slow ascent of the sun, reflecting the exquisite architecture and the serene start of a new day in the city.

➢ **Fifth Avenue Aura**: Choose a rooftop close to the prestigious Fifth Avenue, enveloping yourself in the luxurious spirit of one of the world's most famous streets. Here, the opulence of the surroundings infuses every aspect of your practice, elevating it to a celebration of high urban fashion and timeless grace.

➢ **Colorful Canvases**: Experience the sky as it transforms into a canvas of soft, pastel hues, painting the early morning with colors that enhance the beauty of your surroundings. This natural artwork provides a peaceful and inspiring setting for your yoga session, connecting you deeply with the environment.

- ➢ **Harmonious Heartbeat**: Synchronize your breathing with the subtle yet ever-present pulse of Manhattan. As the city breathes and awakens to a new day, your synchronized breaths foster a deep connection with its dynamic energy, blending inner peace with the city's vibrant life force.

- ➢ **Designer Distinction**: While the designer logo on your yoga mat may signify style, it's the distinctiveness of your poses and the fluidity of your movements that truly capture the attention of any onlooker. Your practice embodies the city's morning magic, overshadowing any branded insignia with the pure artistry of your form.

- ➢ **Urban Energy Infusion**: Draw upon the energetic vibrations of Manhattan, a city famed for its unstoppable pace and vibrant spirit. Let this energy invigorate your yoga practice, fueling your movements with strength and your mind with a heightened sense of awareness and inspiration.

- ➢ **Iconic Inspirations**: Allow the iconic status of your Manhattan backdrop to inspire your yoga journey both spiritually and physically. Each posture and breath becomes a reflective moment, paying tribute to the resilience, beauty, and spirit of Manhattan, encouraging a deeper connection with the city and with yourself.

In "Dawn's Embrace: Yoga with a Manhattan View," we discover a harmonious blend of serenity and ambition. As the iconic skyline unfolds around you, your yoga practice becomes a deep connection to the bustling city. Amidst the skyscrapers and busy streets, you find a personal sanctuary where your spirit syncs with Manhattan's pulse. So, roll out your mats and let the city inspire you. Here, each sunrise isn't just a spectacle—it's an invitation to join in the city's epic story. Welcome to "Dawn's Embrace," where your practice dances with the urban rhythm, and every pose reflects the limitless skyline. Namaste, Manhattan.

Completed Tasks: Dawn's Embrace Activities

Inspirational Quote

THE PEOPLE WHO INFLUENCE YOU ARE THE PEOPLE WHO BELIEVE IN YOU. — Henry Drummond

Action Items: Intentions and Thoughts

The Manhattan Stretch: Crafting Your Urban Flow, Yoga in the Sky

Darlings, join me on a journey where yoga transcends practice and becomes a dance with Manhattan's vibrant pulse. Picture yourself on sky-high terraces, merging seamlessly with the city's energy. Welcome to "The Manhattan Stretch: Crafting Your Urban Flow, Yoga in the Sky," where every pose becomes a masterpiece against the city's grand backdrop.

➢ **Sky-High Serenity**: Ascend to unparalleled peace atop Manhattan's lofty terraces, where the vast cityscape stretches beneath the clouds, offering a tranquil escape on your yoga mat high above the bustling streets. Here, the promise of serenity and solitude rises above the urban chaos, providing a perfect setting for meditation and movement.

➢ **Metropolitan Mastery**: Master the unique discipline of "The Manhattan Stretch," where every yoga pose is not just a physical alignment but a synchronization with the pulsating energy of the city itself. Craft a flow that's distinctly urban, intertwining the rhythm of your breath with the ceaseless vibrancy of Manhattan's heartbeat.

➢ **Pose with Poise**: Allow the grandeur of Manhattan's skyline to inspire your transitions between poses, reflecting the architectural elegance and soaring aspirations of the city. Each movement becomes a tribute to the towering structures and graceful contours that define the metropolis.

➢ **Breathe in the City**: With every inhale, draw in the dynamic energy that Manhattan emits; with every exhale, release the stresses and strains of urban life. Let this breathing practice deepen your connection to the city, allowing its spirited essence to rejuvenate and empower you.

➢ **Elevated Energy**: Experience the exhilaration of practicing yoga with a panoramic view of the city. This elevated perspective not only enhances the physical benefits of each pose but also infuses your practice with a sense of grandeur and possibility, echoing the boundless energy of Manhattan.

➢ **Yoga with a View**: Transform your daily yoga routine into a captivating visual experience. Perform your vinyasa flow with a backdrop that shifts from the iconic Empire State Building to the serene flow of the Hudson River, making your practice a profound connection to the city's most beloved landmarks.

➢ **Artistic Alignment**: Consider each session on the mat as an opportunity to paint a living canvas, with your body as the brush and Manhattan as your color palette. Together, you create a dynamic masterpiece of movement and mindfulness that harmoniously blends with the urban landscape, enhancing your sense of unity with the city.

➢ **Celebrate the Cityscape**: As you conclude your practice, take a moment to deeply appreciate the magnificent city sprawled beneath you. From your final relaxation pose, reflect on the beauty and endless energy of Manhattan that not only uplifts but also profoundly inspires every aspect of your yoga journey, leaving you invigorated and connected to the essence of this iconic city.

In "The Manhattan Stretch," we discover a perfect blend of peace and ambition, echoing Manhattan's iconic skyline. Each yoga pose deepens your connection to the vibrant city, serving as a serene escape within its bustling atmosphere. So, roll out your mats and let the city lift your practice to new heights, where every stretch is a dance with Manhattan's pulse. Namaste, Manhattan.

RISE AND SHINE, MANHATTAN STYLE

Completed Tasks: Yoga in the Sky Activities

Inspirational Quote

I HAVE BEGUN TO THINK OF LIFE AS A SERIES OF RIPPLES WIDENING OUT
FROM AN ORIGINAL CENTER. — Seamus Heaney

Action Items: Intentions and Thoughts

The Manhattan Stretch: Crafting Your Urban Flow, Finding Inner Peace

Darlings, let me whisk you away on a journey where yoga transcends the ordinary and becomes a graceful dance with the vibrant pulse of Manhattan. Welcome to "The Manhattan Stretch: Crafting Your Urban Flow, Finding Inner Peace." Picture practicing yoga on sky-high terraces, where your every pose is a masterpiece against the backdrop of this magnificent metropolis.

> ➢ **Elevated Enlightenment**: Rise above the ordinary with yoga sessions on Manhattan's sky-high terraces, where the awe-inspiring views heighten your sense of clarity and calm. Embrace a practice that lifts your spirit alongside the city's towering skyscrapers, creating a serene high-altitude retreat from the urban rush below.

> ➢ **Cityscape Contemplation**: Amidst the vibrant energy of the city that never sleeps, find your center against a backdrop of bustling streets and iconic architecture. Each yoga pose offers a precious moment of tranquility, allowing you to draw peace from the pulsating energy of Manhattan.

> ➢ **Architectural Alignment**: Let the striking contours of Manhattan's skyline inspire your yoga flow. Align your body and spirit with the structural masterpieces that surround you, finding symmetry and balance in the reflection of urban beauty.

> ➢ **Metropolitan Meditation**: Delve into a deep meditative state that harnesses the dynamic spirit of Manhattan. Transform the city's ceaseless energy into a powerful force for personal rejuvenation and spiritual awakening, making the metropolis your meditation partner.

> ➢ **Skyline Serenity**: Greet the day with Sun Salutations as the sun rises over Manhattan, casting the city in golden hues and inspiring a session filled with warmth and light. Experience the rare serenity

found at the intersection of daybreak and the city skyline, enhancing your connection to both self and surroundings.

➤ **Urban Oasis Yoga**: Discover an urban oasis where you can retreat to perform your yoga routine high above the noise and chaos of street life. In this elevated haven, the city's sounds are a distant murmur, allowing for a concentration and mindfulness that deepens every pose and breath.

➤ **Pose with Panorama**: Elevate your yoga practice with every asana framed by a breathtaking panoramic view of Manhattan. The vastness of your surroundings encourages more profound stretches and more powerful poses, each one enriched by the expanse of the cityscape stretching out beneath you.

➤ **Breath of Fresh Air**: Inhale the crisp, fresh air found at higher altitudes and exhale the weight of everyday city stresses. Your rooftop retreat provides a unique vantage point to connect with Manhattan's spirited ambiance, breathing new life into your practice and reaffirming your bond with the city's dynamic soul.

As we delve into "The Manhattan Stretch," we unlock the exquisite fusion of tranquility and ambition. Your yoga practice becomes a living expression of your connection to this dynamic metropolis, much like the iconic landmarks that grace Manhattan's skyline. In the city's bustling streets and towering skyscrapers, there exists a sanctuary—a place where your soul dances in harmony with the heart of Manhattan. Roll out your mats, my darlings, and let the city inspire you. In Manhattan, every yoga pose invites you not merely to stretch but to soar, and your practice becomes a poetic dance with the urban soul. Namaste, Manhattan. Namaste.

Completed Tasks: Finding Inner Peace Activities

_____

_____

_____

_____

_____

_____

_____

_____

_____

_____

_____

_____

_____

_____

_____

_____

_____

_____

_____

_____

_____

_____

Inspirational Quote

MY LIFE IS MY MESSAGE. — Mahatma Gandhi

YOGA WITH A CITYSCAPE

Action Items: Intentions and Thoughts

Action Items: Intentions and Thoughts

_____
_____
_____
_____
_____
_____
_____
_____
_____
_____
_____
_____
_____
_____
_____
_____
_____
_____
_____
_____
_____
_____
_____
_____
_____
_____
_____
_____

Golden Hour Gratitude:
Reflecting on Manhattan Magic at First Light

Manhattan, a city that doesn't merely awaken—it blossoms, as the first rays of dawn illuminate stories of dreams, dances, and delightful dalliances. Here, between the lanes of lore and boulevards of brimming brilliance, it isn't just about greeting a new day; it's about how you soak in its golden embrace—with gratitude, grace, and a glint of gusto.

Now picture this: You're standing atop a SoHo loft, with the horizon stretching out before you, not because you want to catch the sunrise, but to become one with its golden hue. That, my dear, is the Manhattan Morning Muse, a ritual that's less about the time of day and more about tapping into a reservoir of reflection, shimmering with memories, moments, and the magic of possibility.

In this luminous chapter of The Manhattan Diaries, we'll delve into the sacred space that is the golden hour. From the delicate dance of sunrays on the Hudson to the way they caress the façade of The Chrysler Building, you'll learn to bask not just in the light, but in the love of a city that has watched countless dreams unfold.

Yet, this isn't solely about the hues of dawn—no. It's about feeling the city's heartbeat sync with yours, about finding serenity amidst skyscrapers, and recognizing that with every sunrise, Manhattan doesn't just offer a new day, but a canvas ripe with opportunities. It's about realizing that in the shimmering space between shadow and sunbeam lies the essence of Manhattan's eternal embrace.

So, join me, as we transcend the tangible and float in the ethereal, where the golden hour is not just a moment, but a mood, a memory, a melody. Because, darling, in Manhattan, every sunrise is a symphony of gratitude. And as the city unfurls its luminance, know that it's not just lighting up streets and structures; it's lighting up souls.

Chasing Sunrise: Manhattan's Morning Ritual, Golden Hour Obsession

Darlings, let's embark on a journey through Manhattan's enchanting mornings, where the city's pulse quickens with the first light, and every dawn is a canvas painted with promises. This is "Chasing Sunrise: Manhattan's Morning Ritual, Golden Hour Obsession." Picture standing on a SoHo loft, not merely to catch the sunrise, but to become one with its golden embrace—a ritual where time loses meaning and memories are etched in the hues of daybreak.

➤ **Dawn's First Blush**: Embrace the serene early morning calm as Manhattan gently awakens from its slumber. As the first blush of dawn creeps over the horizon, allow the quiet of the early hours to set the stage for a day brimming with endless possibilities and new beginnings.

➤ **Golden Hour Glamour**: Revel in the enchanting glow of the golden hour, where every building, street, and park in Manhattan is bathed in a soft, luminous light. This magical time transforms the ordinary into the extraordinary, imbuing the cityscape with a dreamlike quality that captures the heart and imagination.

➤ **SoHo Sunrise**: Position yourself atop a stylish SoHo loft and witness the city come alive from one of its most fashionable districts. Here, the skyline unfolds before you in a breathtaking spectacle of light and color, offering a moment of connection between you, the dawn, and the vibrant life below.

➤ **Ritual of Renewal**: Elevate your morning by turning the act of watching the sunrise into a sacred ritual. This is a time to reset and recharge, aligning your inner rhythms with the serene, hopeful energy of the early sky as the city's pulse syncs with the new day.

➢ **Memory Making Moments**: As the sun rises, capture memories that will last a lifetime. Each moment is rendered more picturesque by the radiant dawn, crafting snapshots that encapsulate the beauty of Manhattan mornings—each one worth cherishing forever.

➢ **Timeless Mornings**: Lose yourself in the timeless beauty of a Manhattan sunrise. In these moments, time seems to stand still, the city transforms into a canvas painted with vibrant hues and soft silhouettes, and every sense is engaged in the beauty of daybreak.

➢ **Urban Tranquility**: Discover a unique tranquility in the heart of the urban jungle as the rising sun imparts peace and a fresh perspective on the day ahead. This tranquil experience reminds us of New York City's dual nature—simultaneously bustling and breathtakingly beautiful.

➢ **Celebration of Daybreak**: Participate in the city's daily rebirth, celebrating each new day as Manhattan casts off its nocturnal cloak to don the radiant robes of morning. This celebration of daybreak sets the rhythm for life in the metropolis, inspiring all who watch to start their day with a sense of wonder and anticipation.

As we venture into the realm of "Chasing Sunrise," we unlock the enchantment of Manhattan's morning ritual, where each dawn is a masterpiece waiting to be discovered. In the city's bustling streets and towering skyscrapers, there exists a sanctuary—a place where your soul dances in harmony with the heart of Manhattan. So, my darlings, embrace the golden hour, and let the city inspire you. In Manhattan, every sunrise invites you not merely to witness but to become a part of its magnificent narrative, much like the iconic landmarks that grace this vibrant metropolis. Welcome to "Chasing Sunrise," where your mornings are draped in dreams and dazzle.

Completed Tasks: Golden Hair Obsession Activities

Inspirational Quote

WHEN YOU FAIL, YOU LEARN FROM THE MISTAKES YOU MADE, AND IT
MOTIVATES YOU TO WORK EVEN HARDER. — Natalie Gulbis

Action Items: Intentions and Thoughts

Chasing Sunrise: Manhattan's Morning Ritual, Hudson's Dance

Darlings, let's embark on a journey through Manhattan's enchanting mornings, where the city's pulse quickens with the first light, and every dawn is a canvas painted with promises. This is "Chasing Sunrise: Manhattan's Morning Ritual, Hudson's Dance." Picture standing on a SoHo loft, not merely to catch the sunrise, but to become one with its golden embrace—a ritual where time loses meaning and memories are etched in the hues of daybreak.

➤ **Hudson's Golden Waltz**: Immerse yourself in the mesmerizing dance of dawn as it cascades over the Hudson River. Each morning, the river transforms into a shimmering pathway of liquid gold, reflecting the sky's changing hues and beckoning the city to awaken with its rhythmic flow and radiant light.

➤ **SoHo Sunrise Spectacle**: From the vantage point of a stylish SoHo loft, become one with the sunrise. Watch in awe as the cityscape is bathed in golden light, transforming the ordinary into the spectacular. Here, you're not merely an observer of the sunrise but an active participant in its golden embrace.

➤ **City's Awakening Pulse**: As the first light pierces the city's skyline, feel the palpable increase in Manhattan's pulse. Synchronize your own heartbeat with this accelerated rhythm—a city coming to life, energized by the promise and potential of a new day.

➤ **Canvas of Promises**: Each morning in Manhattan presents a fresh canvas, painted with the delicate hues of daybreak. This daily masterpiece promises new stories and unforgettable memories, waiting to be discovered and cherished in the vast urban landscape.

➤ **Timeless Mornings**: Engage in the timeless ritual of chasing the sunrise, where each moment is elongated and every sense is heightened. The early light washes over the city, cleansing it of yesterday's echoes and offering a pristine tableau for today's endeavors.

➤ **Ethereal Mornings**: Stand amidst the ethereal beauty of dawn, where the sky and city meet in a breathtaking display of light and color. This daily phenomenon turns familiar scenes into awe-inspiring vistas, casting a magical spell over the city's architecture and its inhabitants.

➤ **Memory Making at Daybreak**: Each sunrise over Manhattan is an opportunity to create lasting memories. As the sun ascends, its rays etch vibrant streaks across the cityscape, illuminating moments of beauty and casting long shadows that add depth and drama to the start of your day.

➤ **Serenade of the City**: Let the gentle serenade of the morning envelop you as the quieter sounds of the city blend with the soft whispers of the waking day. This harmonious melody provides a tranquil backdrop to the sunrise, resonating with the soul of Manhattan and offering a peaceful start to the hustle and bustle that lies ahead.

As we venture into the realm of "Chasing Sunrise," we unlock the enchantment of Manhattan's morning ritual, where each dawn is a masterpiece waiting to be discovered. In the city's bustling streets and towering skyscrapers, there exists a sanctuary—a place where your soul dances in harmony with the heart of Manhattan. So, my darlings, embrace the golden hour, and let the city inspire you. In Manhattan, every sunrise invites you not merely to witness but to become a part of its magnificent narrative, much like the iconic landmarks that grace this vibrant metropolis. Welcome to "Chasing Sunrise," where your mornings are draped in dreams and dazzle.

Completed Tasks: Morning Ritual Dance Activities

_____

_____

_____

_____

_____

_____

_____

_____

_____

_____

_____

_____

_____

_____

_____

_____

_____

_____

_____

_____

_____

_____

_____

_____

Inspirational Quote

NOT A SHRED OF EVIDENCE EXISTS IN FAVOR OF THE IDEA THAT LIFE IS SERIOUS. — Brendan Gill

Action Items: Intentions and Thoughts

Manhattan's Eternal Embrace: Finding Serenity Amidst Skyscrapers, Chrysler's Caress

Darlings, join me on a captivating journey through the heart of Manhattan, where the city's timeless embrace offers a sanctuary amidst the towering skyscrapers. This is "Manhattan's Eternal Embrace: Finding Serenity Amidst Skyscrapers, Chrysler's Caress." Picture the city's iconic Chrysler Building bathed in the morning light, a symbol of the enduring love affair between nature and architecture. In Manhattan, serenity is not lost among the bustling streets; it's discovered in the most unexpected places.

- ➢ **Chrysler's Morning Kiss**: Experience the majestic Chrysler Building as it captures the first rays of the morning sun. Watch its iconic art deco spire gleam against the dawn, serving as a beacon of inspiration and a testament to Manhattan's enduring love affair with its architectural heritage.

- ➢ **Urban Sanctuary**: Amidst the hustle and bustle of the city, discover hidden sanctuaries of peace nestled between towering skyscrapers. These quiet corners and serene spaces provide a much-needed retreat from the urban chaos, offering moments of tranquility where you can reconnect with yourself amidst the relentless pace of city life.

- ➢ **Skyline Serenity**: Stand in awe of the stunning Manhattan skyline, where the chaotic beauty of soaring buildings offers a unique form of calm. Each structure, with its own story of dreams and achievements, whispers tales from the past and hopes for the future, inviting you to find a contemplative peace in their towering presence.

- ➢ **Nature Meets Metropolis**: Explore the seamless integration of nature and architecture in Manhattan's design. From lush green spaces tucked away on rooftops to expansive terraces interspersed among glass towers, these urban oases offer fresh air and natural

194

beauty, providing a harmonious balance to the city's steel and concrete.

➢ **Reflections of Resilience**: Admire the reflective facades of Manhattan's skyscrapers as they mirror the ever-changing skies above. These surfaces not only enhance the city's aesthetic appeal but also symbolize its incredible adaptability and resilience, reflecting the dynamic nature of New York life.

➢ **Architectural Affection**: Feel the embrace of the city through its diverse architecture. From the romantic spires of Gothic cathedrals to the sleek lines of modernist towers, each building offers a unique caress that connects you to the pulse of Manhattan, allowing you to physically feel the vibrancy and spirit of the city.

➢ **Whispers of the Waterfront**: Seek solace along the waterfronts of Manhattan, where the East and Hudson Rivers provide a serene backdrop for reflection. The gentle lapping of the waves against the shorelines offers a rhythmic tranquility, syncing perfectly with your inner tempo and providing a meditative space to contemplate and rejuvenate.

➢ **Iconic Interludes**: Take a meaningful pause beneath the towering presence of landmarks like the Chrysler Building. These moments allow you to reflect on the grandeur and history of the city while considering your own narrative within its vast and storied landscape.

In "Manhattan's Eternal Embrace," we find tranquility among the skyscrapers. The Chrysler Building's morning light and the city's artful skyline remind us that serenity exists even in unexpected places. From rooftop havens to Central Park's quiet trails, Manhattan offers moments of peace amidst its vibrant hustle. As you explore, remember that tranquility is discovered, not lost, in the heart of this bustling metropolis. Welcome to a Manhattan where art, love, and peace create a beautiful, enduring tapestry.

Completed Tasks: Building's Caress Activities

_____
_____
_____
_____
_____
_____
_____
_____
_____
_____
_____
_____
_____
_____
_____
_____
_____
_____
_____
_____
_____
_____
_____
_____
_____

Inspirational Quote

REMEMBER, WHEN LIFE'S PATH IS STEEP TO KEEP YOUR MIND EVEN. —
Horace

GOLDEN HOUR GRATITUDE

Action Items: Intentions and Thoughts

Manhattan's Eternal Embrace: Finding Serenity Amidst Skyscrapers, Soulful Sunrise Symphony

Darlings, let's embark on a journey through the heart of Manhattan, where the city's timeless embrace offers a sanctuary amidst the towering skyscrapers. This is "Manhattan's Eternal Embrace: Finding Serenity Amidst Skyscrapers, Soulful Sunrise Symphony." Picture the city's iconic Chrysler Building bathed in the morning light, a symbol of the enduring love affair between nature and architecture. In Manhattan, serenity isn't lost amidst the bustling streets; it's discovered in the most unexpected places, where the soulful symphony of sunrise unfolds.

- ➤ **Skyward Serenity**: Ascend to the serene heights of Manhattan's rooftops where the day begins with a soulful sunrise symphony. Here, amidst the towering skyscrapers, the city's hustle fades into a backdrop of calm, setting a peaceful tone for the day as you're enveloped in the gentle light of dawn.

- ➤ **Chrysler Charm**: Embrace the morning as the iconic Chrysler Building greets the day, bathed in soft morning light. Its gleaming art deco facade serves as a stunning reminder of Manhattan's beautiful blend of architectural ingenuity and natural elegance, standing as a beacon of the city's historical romance with design and detail.

- ➤ **Urban Oasis**: Discover pockets of tranquility within Manhattan's bustling environment. Hidden rooftop gardens and verdant spaces provide a lush, green sanctuary where the air feels fresher and the city's noise dims, offering a peaceful retreat from the urban rush.

- ➤ **Dawn's Early Beauty**: Experience the rare quietude of Manhattan at dawn, when the city takes a deep, restorative breath. This precious time offers a chance to witness the city awaken in softer tones and slower rhythms, allowing you to savor the majestic unfolding of daybreak.

➤ **Architectural Harmony**: Marvel at the harmonious interplay between the city's iconic structures and the rising sun. As the skyline catches the morning rays, each building—from the modern glass towers to the historic brick facades—collaborates to paint a breathtaking scene that underscores the deep connection between urban life and the artistry of nature.

➤ **Reflections of Resilience**: Stand by the reflective waters along the Hudson and East Rivers as they mirror the morning sky. These shimmering surfaces not only showcase the city's resilience and dynamic spirit but also reflect the transformative beauty of daybreak, enhancing the tranquility of your morning.

➤ **Symphony of the Streets**: Listen to the early morning soundscape of Manhattan. The city's awakening is a gentle symphony: the distant hum of awakening commerce, the soft whispers of wind between buildings, and the morning calls of birds in Central Park. Each sound contributes to a unique auditory backdrop that enriches the soulful sunrise.

➤ **Serenity in the Skyline**: Pause to appreciate the skyline as it shifts from the velvety shades of night to the vibrant tones of day. Each building silhouetted against the burgeoning dawn offers a moment of mindfulness, encouraging contemplation and connection with the expansive cityscape that defines Manhattan. This daily transformation is a meditation in itself, inspiring awe and offering a profound sense of place within the vast metropolis.

In "Manhattan's Eternal Embrace," discover serenity amid skyscrapers. The Chrysler Building's morning glow and the city's skyline blend art and nature, offering peaceful moments from rooftops to Central Park. Explore Manhattan's landmarks and find tranquility at the heart of this vibrant city, where art, love, and peace weave a beautiful tapestry.

Completed Tasks: Soulful Sunrises Activities

_____

_____

_____

_____

_____

_____

_____

_____

_____

_____

_____

_____

_____

_____

_____

_____

_____

_____

_____

_____

_____

_____

_____

_____

_____

Inspirational Quote

GO BIG OR GO HOME. BECAUSE IT'S TRUE. WHAT DO YOU HAVE TO LOSE?
— Eliza Dushku

GOLDEN HOUR GRATITUDE

Action Items: Intentions and Thoughts

Action Items: Intentions and Thoughts

_____

_____

_____

_____

_____

_____

_____

_____

_____

_____

_____

_____

_____

_____

_____

_____

_____

_____

_____

_____

_____

_____

_____

_____

_____

_____

_____

City Roundup: City Soiree – A Grand Tour of Manhattan's Daily Delights

Ladies and gentlemen, it's been quite the journey through the pages of "Rise and Shine, Manhattan-Style: Day-to-Day Luxuries You Can't Miss," and now, as we wrap up our literary tour with "City Roundup" I can't help but reflect on the dazzling tapestry that is Manhattan. In this city of dreams, every day unfolds like a chapter in an urban fairytale, where luxury isn't just about the lavish, but about the profound experiences that shape our souls.

Throughout our exploration, we've sipped coffee in hidden cafes, danced through the city's historic streets, savored gourmet breakfasts, found solace in sunrise yoga, and witnessed the golden hour's magic. We've uncovered the secrets of fashion, the artistry of avocado toast, and the allure of hidden gems. We've marveled at the city's iconic landmarks, from Central Park's verdant embrace to the Chrysler Building's morning caress.

But beyond the glamour and the glitz, Manhattan has whispered its mysteries to us.

It's a city that demands you not just to exist but to thrive, to unravel your inner self in the grand tapestry of its streets. From the shimmering skyscrapers to the serene moments in the park, Manhattan has shown us that luxury is also about finding tranquility amidst the chaos, about connecting with nature in the heart of a metropolis, and about tapping into the rhythms of your soul while dancing to the city's beat.

As we conclude our journey through "Rise and Shine, Manhattan-Style," remember that the true luxuries of life aren't always material; they're the experiences that shape us, the moments that leave an indelible mark on our hearts. Manhattan has taught us that in the midst of its grandeur, it's in the simple pleasures and profound discoveries that we truly find ourselves.

So, my dear readers, carry these Manhattan mystiques with you as you continue your own unique journeys. The city may never sleep, but it also never stops inspiring, revealing, and challenging us to become the best versions of ourselves. And isn't that the ultimate luxury of all?

Rise and Shine, Manhattan Style Recap Checklist

The Manhattan Diaries program series recap checklist—completes step eight of your 21 step journey. Think of this program as a time release supplement that does its magic over the course of 21 steps, days, or weeks—you set your schedule. By committing to one chapter each morning—or one book each day or week; in 21 short days or weeks you will be able to change your life into a new You. In this book, we covered:

1. Penthouse Perspectives: Sunrise Meditations Amidst Skyscrapers

In "Penthouse Perspectives: Sunrise Meditations Amidst Skyscrapers" from The Manhattan Diaries, we explore the enriching experience of meditating at dawn atop Manhattan's penthouses. Beyond the luxury, it delves into a deep connection with the city's awakening—where skyscrapers are more than buildings; they're guardians of dreams, and their shadows tell hidden stories. This chapter invites readers to experience a meditation that intertwines personal tranquility with the vibrant pulse of Manhattan, making each sunrise a masterpiece that uplifts the soul.

2. Café Society: The Art of the Manhattan Morning Latte Ritual

In "Café Society: The Art of the Manhattan Morning Latte Ritual" from The Manhattan Diaries, we explore the cherished morning coffee tradition in Manhattan. Set in a charming café off Madison Avenue, this narrative celebrates the ritual where the steam rising from a morning latte becomes a symbol of personal connection to the city's vibrant pulse. More than just a drink, each latte is a crafted expression of ambition and elegance, weaving the drinker's story with Manhattan's dynamic spirit. This chapter highlights how a simple morning beverage transforms into a meaningful rite of passage, encapsulating the essence of Manhattan in every sip.

3. The Silk Robe Affair: Embracing Morning Glamour, Room with a View

In "The Silk Robe Affair: Embracing Morning Glamour, Room with a View" from The Manhattan Diaries, we dive into the indulgent world of morning glamour on Manhattan's Upper East Side. The chapter describes the luxurious experience of starting the day in a silk robe, overlooking the cityscape. It emphasizes how such mornings go beyond daily routines, blending personal elegance with the panoramic city views to create a ritual that stirs the soul. This narrative explores the transformative power of these morning rituals, where every element—from the silk's caress to the skyline at dawn—enhances the allure of Manhattan's vibrant lifestyle.

4. Manhattan Mantras: Uplifting Affirmations for City Divas

In "Manhattan Mantras: Uplifting Affirmations for City Divas" from The Manhattan Diaries, the chapter explores the power of affirmations in enhancing life in bustling Manhattan. It highlights how these affirmations strengthen style and confidence, from serene, candle-lit moments to declarations atop city rooftops. Readers learn to synchronize their affirmations with their own rhythm and the city's pace, demonstrating how these mantras connect them deeply with Manhattan and facilitate significant personal empowerment.

5. Fifth Avenue Facials: Starting the Day with a Fresh Face and Fabulous Glow

In "Fifth Avenue Facials: Starting the Day with a Fresh Face and Fabulous Glow" from The Manhattan Diaries, we delve into Manhattan's facial treatments that epitomize the city's luxury and meticulous beauty culture. This chapter uncovers the transformative facials at exclusive salons and hidden spas, showcasing how these rituals are an integral part of a glamorous Manhattan lifestyle. More than mere maintenance, they equip residents with the confidence to face their day, proving that a morning facial is not just a routine but a crucial indulgence for anyone in the city that never sleeps.

6. Central Park Serenades: Early Morning Walks with the City's Heartbeat

In "The Breakfast Club: Gourmet Beginnings in the City that Never Sleeps" from The Manhattan Diaries, we dive into Manhattan's breakfast scene where the meal becomes a glamorous event. This chapter guides readers through an array of gourmet breakfast spots, from exquisite pancake stacks to artisanal coffee shops, highlighting not just the food but the whole experience. It captures the essence of morning rituals in Manhattan, where breakfast is a moment to savor the city's awakening and luxuriate in its vibrant beginnings. Join us on this culinary journey where each morning offers a chance to partake in the city's grand narrative, one delicious bite at a time.

7. The Breakfast Club: Gourmet Beginnings in the City that Never Sleeps

In "The Breakfast Club: Gourmet Beginnings in the City that Never Sleeps" from The Manhattan Diaries, we explore Manhattan's luxurious breakfast scene. This chapter showcases a variety of gourmet spots, from pancake houses to artisanal coffee shops, highlighting not just the food but the overall experience. It presents breakfast as a cherished ritual that captures the vibrancy of Manhattan's morning. Dive into this culinary journey where each meal is an opportunity to experience the city's dynamic atmosphere, one delicious bite at a time.

8. Dawn's Designer Diary: Crafting a Day's Ensemble with Panache

"Dawn's Designer Diary: Crafting a Day's Ensemble with Panache" in The Manhattan Diaries explores how Manhattan's fashion scene is more than just wearing clothes—it's a performance. This chapter delves into how New Yorkers curate outfits that tell stories and capture attention, emphasizing that fashion is a bold, public statement. It guides readers through choosing pieces from hidden vintage boutiques to contemporary designers, illustrating how each ensemble is not just worn but performed to resonate with the city's dynamic rhythm.

9. Yoga with a Cityscape: Stretching to the Skyline's Tune

In "Yoga with a Cityscape: Stretching to the Skyline's Tune" from The Manhattan Diaries, the chapter explores the integration of yoga with the vibrant backdrop of Manhattan's skyline. It emphasizes how rooftop sessions near Fifth Avenue combine physical postures with the city's dynamic pulse, creating a tranquil yet energizing experience. This piece highlights how urban yoga transcends traditional practice, transforming Manhattan's rhythm into a powerful muse for both physical and spiritual growth.

10. Golden Hour Gratitude: Reflecting on Manhattan Magic at First Light

In "Golden Hour Gratitude: Reflecting on Manhattan Magic at First Light" from The Manhattan Diaries, the chapter explores the serene moments of dawn in Manhattan. It describes standing atop a SoHo loft, deeply connecting with the city as the first light illuminates iconic landmarks like the Hudson

River and the Chrysler Building. This time is portrayed as a sacred opportunity for reflection and gratitude, where each sunrise presents a fresh canvas of possibilities, spiritually and emotionally enriching those who experience it.

Where Do We Go From Here?

Where do we go from here? It's a question that lingers in the air like a whispered secret, my dear readers, as we conclude our journey through "Manhattan Vitality: Just Like That." In the heart of Manhattan, where every sunrise brings new opportunities, and each corner reveals hidden gems, it's only natural to contemplate what lies ahead.

As we bid farewell to "Rise and Shine, Manhattan-Style: Day-to-Day Luxuries You Can't Miss," and prepare to delve into "Soul of the City: Unlocking Serenity Amid NYC's Hustle," let's remember that our path through these pages is much like our path through life—an exploration of self, an unraveling of mysteries, and a continuous evolution.

The Manhattan Diaries have been our guides, showing us that in the midst of a bustling metropolis, we can find serenity, luxury, and a deeper connection to ourselves. It's about embracing the vitality of Manhattan, not just in its grandeur but in its everyday moments.

So, where do we go from here? We go forward, my darlings, with open hearts and open minds. We embrace the vibrancy of the city, savor the luxuries it offers, and unlock the secrets it holds. We continue our journey of self-discovery, knowing that every step, every sunrise, and every page turned in The Manhattan Diaries brings us closer to unraveling our inner selves in the most extraordinary of ways.

Completed Tasks: Recap Checklist Activities

_____

_____

_____

_____

_____

_____

_____

_____

_____

_____

_____

_____

_____

_____

_____

_____

_____

_____

_____

_____

_____

_____

_____

_____

_____

_____

_____

_____

_____

_____

Inspirational Quote

DON'T GIVE UP. DON'T LOSE HOPE. DON'T SELL OUT. — Christopher Reeve

Action Items: Intentions and Thoughts

Journal Pages: Pen Your Tales

Journal Pages: Pen Your Tales

Journal Pages: Pen Your Tales

Journal Pages: Pen Your Tales

Journal Pages: Pen Your Tales

Journal Pages: Pen Your Tales

Journal Pages: Pen Your Tales

Journal Pages: Pen Your Tales

Journal Pages: Pen Your Tales

Journal Pages: Pen Your Tales

www.ingramcontent.com/pod-product-compliance
Lightning Source LLC
Chambersburg PA
CBHW021622120626
46545CB00001B/349